Hand in Hand with God

CW01653923

Inspiring
Women
to go deeper with God

Hand in Hand with God

Finding hope in a hurting world

Jeannette Barwick and Beverley Shepherd

Foreword by Wendy Virgo

CWR

Copyright © CWR 2005
Published 2005 by CWR, Waverley Abbey House, Waverley Lane, Farnham, Surrey GU9 8EP, England.

The rights of Jeannette Barwick and Beverley Shepherd to be identified as the authors of this work have been asserted by them in accordance with the Copyright, Designs and Patents Act 1988, sections 77 and 78.

All rights reserved. No part of this publication may be reproduced, stored in a retrieval system, or transmitted, in any form or by any means, electronic, mechanical, photocopying, recording or otherwise, without the prior permission in writing of CWR.

See back of book for list of National Distributors.

Unless otherwise indicated, all Scripture references are from the Holy Bible: New International Version (NIV), copyright © 1973, 1978, 1984 by the International Bible Society.
Other versions used are marked:
Amp: The Amplified Bible Old Testament copyright © 1965, 1987 by the Zondervan Corporation. The Amplified New Testament copyright © 1958 by the Lockman Foundation. Used by permission.
NKJV: New King James Version, © 1982, Thomas Nelson Inc.
The Message: *The Message*, by Eugene Peterson, copyright © 1993, 1994, 1995, 1996, 2000, 2001, 2002. Used by permission of NavPress Publishing Group.

Concept development, editing, design and production by CWR
Front cover image: Artville: Don Bishop
Printed in Malta by Progress Press Ltd
ISBN: 1-85345-367-6

Contents

Meet the Women at Waverley Team

Jeannette Barwick, founder of CWR's Ministry to Women, has long been committed to helping women apply biblical principles to their lives and relationships. In 1987, the first event for women was held at Waverley Abbey House and over the years the heart of Waverley's teaching for women has been shared around the world through seminars, events and publications. Jeannette also teaches on temperament differences and co-ordinates Selwyn Hughes' worldwide ministry.

Beth Clark, the most senior member of the team, is a lady whose life is steeped in the Scriptures. Her Bible study has been ongoing for nearly 30 years and her workshops on Bible Meditation at Women at Waverley weekends are greatly prized. She has endeared herself to all who know her, not only by her humility and prayerfulness, but also by her remarkable ability to establish rapport with people of all ages.

Beverley Shepherd has been a team member for over ten years. She is involved in varied and demanding work as a training consultant. The encouraging and equipping of Christians in the workplace is one of her passions, and she is an associate speaker for the London Institute of Contemporary Christianity headed by Mark Greene. She brings to the team verve and vitality as well as depth of biblical understanding, and is especially appreciated for her ability to relate biblical truth to contemporary issues, particularly as they impact women.

Nicky-Sue Leonard is a a gifted teacher and a relative newcomer to the team, bringing to it her expertise and experience as a CWR-trained counsellor and facilitator of post-abortion workshops based on Christian principles. For a number of years she has co-ordinated women's events at Waverley and around the UK. Apart from an expanding role as a speaker at women's events, she is increasingly involved in teaching on CWR's counselling courses.

Foreword

I love the book of Ruth! It has everything: pathos and grief, loyalty and friendship, a blossoming romance threatened with obstacles, and – sigh of relief – a happy ending! But of course, what makes it so compelling for the Christian woman is that it is true, and more than that, it contains truth applicable to us.

Jeannette and Beverley have created a little gem of a book. I only wish I had been present at the original teaching days to hear their wisdom first hand. But now we can read and digest at our leisure the distilled wisdom of these godly teachers as they unfold for us Naomi and Ruth's relationship which led one lonely, aching woman into ultimate serenity and contentment, and the other, an alien from a foreign nation, to find refuge under the wings of the Almighty, and love and security under the cloak of a loving husband.

How appropriate are these elements for women in our own day! In these times of movement of people around the globe, many feel estranged from their own cultures, and struggle to find a foothold and acceptance in an adopted country. As nation rises against nation, increased tensions lead to reluctance to befriend, unwillingness to accept. Yet this is the heart of the gospel: to welcome the stranger, to make room for the outcast. 'When I was hungry, you fed me, when I was a stranger, you took me in,' said Jesus. Naomi, wrapped in the gloom of triple bereavement, nevertheless accepted her Moabite daughter-in-law, and found that her own depressed heart became light as she became caught up in Ruth's story.

Ruth's beautiful words of commitment to Naomi echo through the centuries, repeated at weddings, used as a model to declare undying loyalty. Then what a picture Boaz portrays of the kinsman-redeemer who takes the foreigner under his protection, paying the price in order to make her his own, and then uniting with her in marriage.

Some women will identify with Naomi as she goes from one incredible hardship to another, all of which conspire to make her a woman bitter and turned in on herself. Yet Ruth refuses to leave her to her depression, sticks to her like a limpet, and truly respects her. Ultimately Naomi comes out from the shadows into light and joy.

This is a book showing the power of covenant love. It gently leads the reader through into an understanding of this love whereby she can enter into the blessings of it for herself. It will enrich many lives. I love it, and I know you will too!

Wendy Virgo

Introduction

This book reflects the heart of the teaching from a Women at Waverley weekend of spiritual refreshing. The focus of our fellowship one particular weekend was the book of Ruth, a book of only four short chapters but, nevertheless, a fast-moving and classic tale that grips readers with its drama and delights them with its happy ending. Through the lives of two fascinating women, Naomi and Ruth, we gain fresh insights of our great and loving God who seeks always to draw us closer to Himself, daily putting before us 'handfuls on purpose'. We learn how to look for these tokens of His goodness – encouraging surprises, new and exciting disclosures of His grace – and how to enjoy the serendipity of His love. Understanding the covenant love and faithfulness of our loving God to His people, collectively and individually, encourages us to see our place within God's purposes today.

I vividly remember the occasion when this theme was first explored with women over a weekend at Waverley Abbey House. It was autumn and for two weeks much of the UK had experienced torrential rain, some areas being extensively flooded. Indeed, on the Monday afternoon of the previous week, Waverley could only be accessed by a high four-wheel drive vehicle as the lake had overflowed the driveway. However, on Friday, the weather began to clear and, on Saturday, it seemed as if God had drawn back the curtains of cloud: the sun shone and we women could stroll and sit in the grounds in the afternoon. On Sunday morning, as we considered our wonderful covenant relationship with God, a dazzling rainbow arched over the House and grounds and we thrilled at this sign of the promise of His unfailing covenantal love. In the afternoon, as we left to make our way home, the clouds began to gather again but the memory of the rainbow remained with us. Waverley Abbey House is a special place where God's peace and presence are felt in a beautiful way, never more so than on this occasion. This natural event powerfully enhanced the times of teaching, worship and fellowship we had experienced over the weekend.

Once more, Beverley Shepherd has joined me in compiling this book so that many more women can experience some of the discoveries we made as we ministered with other members of the Women at Waverley team that weekend. Over the past decade, God has brought together a team of women who delight in ministering to the growing number of women who gather at Waverley to take 'time out' from the busyness of their everyday lives and go deeper with God. Our prayer is that you, too, will take time out, with friends or as a personal retreat, using the thoughts in this little book to experience, as we did, a time of spiritual refreshing.

Jeannette Barwick
Waverley Abbey House
June 2005

Chapter One

In the Days When the Judges Ruled ...

Beverley Shepherd

'In those days Israel had no king;
everyone did as he saw fit ...'

(Judg. 17:6)

The book of Ruth, sandwiched between the Old Testament books of Judges and 1 Samuel, is a love story. As women, the thought of studying such a book naturally warms us, yet, if we look at it as a love story between Ruth and Boaz only, we will miss much of its richness. It is part of the ongoing love story of God for His people; it challenges us to examine how we live in a society that has turned away from God. The very heartbeat of this book is covenantal love and faithfulness – between God and His people and between individuals. Yes, Ruth is a love story – but it is a love story that embraces your life and mine as we seek to be part of God's salvation purposes for this world. It is a love story that reveals something of the heart of God for us – His people.

The book of Ruth is carefully crafted by its unknown author – every word is there for a reason. Also, Ruth is unique in the Bible for being a story told from an almost exclusively feminine perspective and as such it offers us a window into the usually invisible and private world of the women of the ancient world.

The time

'Once upon a time' is the age-old formula for our children's stories – placing them beyond time and free of context. Yet the story of Ruth starts, 'In the days when the judges ruled …'. This sets it somewhere between 1380 and 1050 BC, ie after the Exodus out of Egypt and entry into the promised land, but before the era of the kings – Saul, David, Solomon, etc. It was a time when judges were appointed to lead Israel and save them from their enemies.

The context

Throughout the book of Judges there are two refrains. The first is: 'Again the Israelites did evil in the eyes of the LORD' (Judg. 3:7, 12; 4:1; 6:1; 10:6; 13:1). Each of these refrains introduces the cycle of rebellion, oppression, distress and deliverance that is outlined in Judges 2:

> Whenever the LORD raised up a judge for them, he was with the judge and saved them out of the hands of their enemies as long as the judge lived; for the LORD had compassion on them as they groaned under those who oppressed and afflicted them. But when the judge died, the people returned to ways even more corrupt than those of their fathers, following other gods and serving and worshipping them. They refused to give up their evil practices and stubborn ways.
>
> (Judg. 2:18–19)

God repeatedly brings judgment on His people because of this evil by giving their enemies victory over them and, as at the start of the book of Ruth, through famine.

The second refrain found throughout the book of Judges is 'In those days Israel had no king; everyone did as he saw fit' (Judg.17:6; 21:25). The people developed a 'pick 'n' mix' attitude to spirituality – worship of Yahweh, the one true God, was mixed with idolatry and pagan religions to produce an ungodly cocktail. The lack of true godliness in people's homes was reflected in unfaithfulness in relationships, violence on the streets, women being raped and an ailing economy.

The place

The story in the book of Ruth takes place in Bethlehem and in Moab, and a strange contrast is drawn between them by the author. Bethlehem (meaning 'House of Bread', or 'the place of God's provision') is experiencing a famine. This town, where later the King of kings wold be born, was under His judgment for its idolatry and evil practices – in Ruth 2:22 Naomi warns Ruth that Bethlehem is not a safe place for a woman on her own. No wonder there is no bread in the House of Bread!

Moab (meaning 'nothingness') however, is experiencing a time of plenty. Elimelech, Naomi and their two sons find food and a welcome in Moab – they become integrated in Moabite society, intermarrying with the local girls and staying much longer than the 'for a while' that verse 1 suggests. Yet Moab is dubious territory for the people of God with no Moabite being allowed to enter the assembly of the Lord (Deut. 23:3–6). The Moabites worshipped Chemosh – a god who required child sacrifice.

The man

The author zeros in on one family – mum, dad and two boys. The man is Elimelech, meaning 'My God is King'. This man's very name declared the truth that Israel did have a king, despite the refrain of Judges, and that that king was God. Elimelech is living in an age (not unlike our own) where the kingship of God has been rejected (1 Sam. 8:6–7). The author subtly poses the questions: 'Will this man live up to his name, or will he go with the prevailing culture and do what he sees fit in his own eyes?', 'Will he walk by faith or by sight?' and 'Will he trust God to save him and his family, or will he be self-reliant?'

Unfortunately Ruth 1:1 leads us to the conclusion that this man, despite his name, does not follow the advice of Proverbs 3:5 to 'Trust in the LORD with all your heart and lean not on your own understanding …' Instead he takes matters into his own hands, ignores the warnings against Moab in Deuteronomy and moves his family to Moab. The continuing story supports this conclusion as he and his sons die – presumably the fate they were hoping to escape in Bethlehem. To further emphasise this, the whole town is stirred and recognises Naomi when she eventually returns to Bethlehem with

Ruth (1:19) – so few, if any, had died. There may not have been plenty in the place of God's provision – but there was enough!

Through the names of Elimelech's two sons the author is, perhaps, giving us a further insight into the character of this man. One son was called Mahlon, meaning 'weakling', and the other son Kilion, meaning 'sickly'. In Old Testament times, children were seen as your fruit, and in Matthew 7:16–19 Jesus tells His disciples that 'By their fruit you will recognise them ... every good tree bears good fruit, but a bad tree bears bad fruit. A good tree cannot bear bad fruit, and a bad tree cannot bear good fruit.' By telling us the names of Elimelech's sons we learn that this man does not produce good fruit that will last (see John 15), and as in Matthew 7:19, his life is cut down.

Elimelech becomes a symbol for the whole Israelite nation – a nation called and chosen by God their King to live obedient fruitful lives in trusting dependence on their Lord. Yet, like Elimelech, God's people have disowned their God and pursued a life of disobedience and compromise, leading to the nothingness of Moab. And with wonderful irony it will be the submission and faithfulness of a Moabite widow called Ruth who will model to the Israelites what it means for God to be our King!

The challenge

It is all too easy to point the finger of criticism at Elimelech and fail to realise that that leaves three fingers pointing back at us! In the first two verses of the book of Ruth we are faced with the same questions as Elimelech: 'Will we live up to our name of "Christians" – meaning "little Christs", or will we go with the prevailing culture and do what seems fit in our own eyes?', 'Will we trust God to save us and our family, or will we be self-reliant?' and 'Will we walk by faith or by sight?' When faced with a seeming deficiency in God's provision and in the context of a godless society, is our answer any different from that of Elimelech – to place our trust somewhere other than in God?

I want to suggest that there are three main 'objects' of faith that we can be tempted to rely on other than God. These are:

1. The 'seen'
2. Our 'supporters'
3. My 'self'

1. The 'seen'

Hebrews 11:1 tells us that '… faith is being sure of what we hope for and certain of what we do not see'. In fact, the whole book of Hebrews is written to Christians who were tempted to go back to the tangibility of the Jewish faith with its earthly Temple, priesthood and animal sacrifices, telling them that the intangibility of our heavenly Temple and our unseen High Priest who was the final sacrifice, is far, far *better*.

Yet we are no different from those early Christians. We too want to walk by sight and love the tangibility of our material possessions, bank balances and insurance policies. As someone who is self-employed, I am most challenged by this when my work diary for a few months ahead looks empty. Should I trust that God will provide work as and when it is needed? Should I embark on a rapid marketing exercise? Do I panic, or take the situation to God and await His leading for the next step (which may include some marketing)? I remember one December/January period when there was no work, though I had work booked in from February onwards. My first response was to try to fill the gap, phoning existing clients. However, even if they did book work for that period, it then got cancelled. Eventually I got the message – God had another agenda for those two months. It was only as I became still, stopped longing for the tangibility of a full diary and waited on God, that I was in a place to hear what that agenda was. His agenda could not be 'seen' by me and by others in the way confirmed bookings in my diary can, but it was certainly *better*.

Ruth's decision-making is contrasted with Elimelech's for us later on in chapter 1. If she had been walking by sight then Moab would have been her best choice – it provided her best chance of marriage as Naomi spells out in Ruth 1:8–13 and marriage meant financial security, status and provision for old age through your children. Instead, Ruth chooses to go to Bethlehem which, on the face of it, will mean none of those things. Yet Ruth chooses to walk by faith in the living God and entrusts her future to Him, in a way that Elimelech failed to do. The result was certainly *better*!

It is not blind faith that I am advocating here, but a faith that acknowledges the facts as Abraham did and yet trusts in our God who is bigger than the circumstances of our lives.

> Without weakening in his faith, [Abraham] faced the fact that his body was as good as dead – since he was about a hundred years old – and that Sarah's womb was also dead. Yet he did not waver through unbelief regarding the promise of God, but was strengthened in his faith and gave glory to God, being fully persuaded that God had power to do what he had promised.
>
> (Rom. 4:19–21)

Are you and I fully persuaded that God has power to do what He has promised?

2. Our 'supporters'

When I run stress management courses I encourage delegates to think about their support network – those people who can give emotional, practical, intellectual or spiritual support when the need arises. One of the wonderful benefits of being part of the Christian family should be that we provide each other with loving practical assistance. Yet, when we always turn to the same group of family and friends to meet our needs, instead of to God, it is good to examine where our faith really is. One way of examining this is to check our reactions when, for whatever reason, friends are not there for us. Are we distraught, angry, hurt or feeling let down? Or do we trust that God's provision for our situation will be met in ways as yet unseen?

A few years ago I decided to move house – a move that I had been thinking about for a while but became definite in my mind when a lovely cottage in my village came on the market. I offered the asking price, but so did someone elase and we were put in a contracts race. I had set my heart on this cottage and so when the survey showed up subsidence in a small extension and the solicitor uncovered a potential legal difficulty, I was still determined to go ahead. I felt very alone in all of this and 'complained' to God that he should have provided someone to stand with me in this difficult situation. Immediately the faces of my surveyor and solicitor came into my mind – it was as if God was saying, 'Here is my provision for you – I haven't left you alone and without help. Now will you please listen to them! I did, and pulled out of the purchase. Two days later I found the wonderful cottage in which I now live. God is our support and His support is often mediated through other people – but not always the people we think!

> Do not be anxious about anything, but in everything, by prayer and petition, with thanksgiving, present your requests to God. And the peace of God, which transcends all understanding, will guard your hearts and your minds in Christ Jesus.
>
> (Phil. 4:6–7)

3. My 'self'

Many of us have been told that 'God helps those who help themselves'. Although providing a helpful corrective to laziness and passivity this statement is a lie – the people God helps are not those who are self-reliant but those who are God-dependent. Being self-reliant can cloak a lack of trust in God, His provision and His timing as Isaiah 50:10–11 emphasises:

> Who among you fears the LORD and obeys the word of his servant? Let [her] who walks in the dark, who has no light, trust in the name of the LORD and rely on [her] God. But now, all you who light fires and provide yourselves with flaming torches, go, walk in the light of your fires and of the torches you have set ablaze. This is what you shall receive from my hand: You will lie down in torment.

God has had to challenge me greatly in this area. In the past (and sometimes now!) I have not been someone who willingly allowed others to see my vulnerability or neediness and would only ask for help as a last resort. Often this mentality masks a deep-seated pride in our own ability to cope. This 'stiff upper lip', 'I'm fine' attitude can spill over into our relationship with God. The difficulty is that we have often been 'rewarded' for this by others – we are the strong ones that people turn to in times of crisis, the world's 'copers', and are admired as such. Things began to change for me when it was lovingly pointed out by a wise Christian friend that the root of this 'I'm fine' attitude is self-reliance and ultimately self-idolatry, that is, a greater trust in my own self-help mechanisms than in God's care for me. Thankfully, for even this, Christ died, so that my artificial self-sufficiency is nailed to the cross of His all-sufficient sacrifice.

Here again Ruth is an example to us – she willingly entrusts herself to the Lord, the God of Israel and shelters under His wings (Ruth 2:12) and in addition she is not too proud to admit her own and Naomi's need for food and receive charity by gleaning in the field of a stranger. So let us follow her example and learn increasingly to walk by faith in the Almighty and not by sight.

As we journey together through the rest of this Old Testament book I pray that each of us will learn increasingly to trust in the provision and protection of our almighty God, and, like Ruth, respond by showing faithful loving commitment to our Lord and to others.

Questions for reflection

- In what ways does the era of the judges compare with the society and values of today?

- What difficulties do the values of today's society pose for us as Christians?

- In what situations are you tempted to rely on 'the seen' more than on God?

- In what situations are you tempted to rely on 'your supporters' more than on God?

- In what situations are you tempted to rely on 'yourself' more than on God?

- Do you need to repent of self-sufficiency? (If your answer to this is 'No, I'm fine!', just stay with this question a little while longer!)

- How does Ruth's willingness to walk by faith and not by sight challenge you?

Chapter Two

Naomi or Mara?

Jeannette Barwick

Based on sessions originally given by Beth Clark

"'Don't call me Naomi,' she told them. 'Call me Mara, because the Almighty has made my life very bitter. I went away full, but the LORD has brought me back empty.'"

(Ruth 1:20)

One of the most important lessons we can learn in life is that God has mysterious purposes even in the greatest of trials. This point comes across with crystal clarity as we look more deeply into the lives of Naomi and Ruth.

Ruth is one of only two books of the Bible named after a woman, the other being Esther. Those who wrote the story down could never have dreamed that, thousands of years later, translated into hundreds of different languages, it would have been read by millions of people. Beverley spoke in the first chapter of this as 'a love story that embraces your life and mine as we seek to be part of God's salvation purposes for this world' and I believe that the lives of Naomi and Ruth most certainly do have meaning and relevance for our lives today. Romans 15:4 (NKJV) tells us, 'For whatever things were written before were written for our learning, that we through the patience and comfort of the Scriptures might have hope' – that we might find hope in our hurting world. In *The Message* by Eugene Peterson that verse is paraphrased as 'Even if it was written in Scripture long ago, you can be sure it's written for us'. So the Bible is telling our story too!

When you and I believingly receive the biblical story we are drawn into the action and find ourselves caught up in the saving movement of God. Philip Greenslade, on whose insights I am also drawing in this chapter, says 'by faith, we can trade in the self-written scripts of our own self-directed lives in order to be written into the larger script of God's big story'.

Death, loss and widowhood

We have seen that in going to Moab things did not work out well for Naomi. Elimelech had died (v.3), her two sons had married Moabite women and then they too died (vv.4–5). Nothing seemed to work well for Naomi. It was probably not the right decision for the family to go to Moab and yet the rest of the story reveals that God has purposes in the greatest of tragedies. He is even able to take our mistakes and turn them around for good. As a result of Elimelech's dubious decision and all that ensued, God's appointed king, David, turned out to be part-Gentile in ancestry. His great-grandmother was Ruth the Moabitess and she is mentioned in the genealogy of Jesus in chapter 1 of Matthew's Gospel. God is able and delights to overrule in distressing situations.

When we see good coming out of something bad, we must never assume that God willed it that way in the first place, but rather that He works through the bad to make all things contribute to His glory. We should never try to foresee the results of an action and thus justify going against God's commands. Instead it should be our practice to decide everything on the basis of God's will as displayed in His Word.

But what an incredible truth it is that He can step into the midst of tragedy and work wonders! For those who are in His purpose He is able to work all things together for good. 'And we know that in all things God works for the good of those who love him, who have been called according to his purpose' (Rom. 8:28).

With her husband and sons dead, Naomi must have felt her life was a write-off, a total loss, BUT God … The Lord was her chief possession. We experience many situations in life where we can say – *but* God. If you circle the many '*but* God' statements as you come across them in the Bible, you will see the God who turns things around in an amazing way.

Take, for example, the story of Joseph as told from chapter 37 onwards in the book of Genesis: how his brothers were jealous of him and sold him into slavery telling their father that he had been killed; how God's hand was on Joseph's life preserving him in many difficult and complex situations; how He kept him strong in the midst of trials and worked everything for good until the day when Joseph, from his position of great authority as Pharaoh's Chief Steward, having met his brothers again, says to them, 'You intended to harm me, *but God* intended it for good to accomplish what is now being done, the saving of many lives' (50:20, my italics). Joseph kept his faith and trust in God and found himself caught up in God's epic story for all mankind.

The Lord's hand is against me

Naomi takes centre stage in chapter 1 of the book of Ruth. Why should she be called upon to suffer so much? First she is afflicted with famine and then she is uprooted from her home and friends to go and live in Moab, an alien culture. Next her husband dies and, within the next few years, she loses both her sons. For a woman in that society the loss of her men folk meant not only the deep pain of bereavement but also the loss of her status, her means of provision and her role – she would be thrown onto the charity of strangers. Naomi had gone to Moab full, but returns empty to Bethlehem. Five times she acknowledges it was the Lord who had afflicted her, and no wonder she declares:

- '… the LORD's hand has gone out against me!' (1:13)
- '… the Almighty has made my life very bitter' (1:20)
- '… the LORD has brought me back empty' (1:21)
- 'The LORD has afflicted me …' (1:21)
- '… the Almighty has brought misfortune on me' (1:21)

Yet here are the very seeds of hope: ultimately these are statements of God's sovereignty. Naomi still sees God as both Lord and Almighty. She recognises God's hand in it all. She speaks easily about God because He is real to her.

Where is God in our pain?

I wonder if you, like Naomi, might be battered by circumstances and suffering great loss? God is still in control. There is Someone to whom you can address your anguished questions: Why? How long? Do You care? Have You forgotten to be merciful? God answers our questions, not just with words, but with the cross. The cross of Christ is a visual aid through which the message comes, 'I love you deeply, My mercy is unfailing. I know and share your pain and anguish.' The Christian life is not trouble-free – we experience the same hardships as non-believers and it is right that we should grieve. Yet we do so in the knowledge of His sovereignty and in the security of His mercy. More than this, we know that God shares in our suffering and comforts us in our loss.

- He promises never to leave us and shares all our rigors and trials (Isa. 41:10; 63:9)
- He has shared fully in our experiences of weakness and pain (Heb. 4:14–15)
- The God of all comfort who comforts us in all our afflictions (2 Cor. 1:3–4)

No, God has not forgotten to be merciful as Naomi is to discover. When she decides to return to Bethlehem (1:8), she says to her two daughters-in-law, 'Go back, each of you, to your mother's home. May the LORD show kindness to you, as you have shown to your dead and to me.' Orpah tearfully says goodbye to her mother-in-law but Ruth goes with Naomi.

When Naomi arrived back in Bethlehem, she was welcomed by the whole community who, it seems, turned out in force to greet her. In verse 19 they say, 'Can this be Naomi?' so a change must have taken place in her appearance. Naomi's response is swift and tinged with self-recrimination, 'Don't call me Naomi [meaning sweet or pleasant] … Call me Mara [unpleasant], because the Almighty has made my life very bitter. I went away full, but the LORD has brought me back empty.' Naomi could not bear the contradiction between the name she bore and the woman she was.

Naomi or Mara? Things may happen in our lives, for some of which we are responsible, others for which we are not. There is a sense in which we all choose whether to allow those things to make us bitter or better.

A redeemed people

A wonderful story of redemption is played out through the relationships of Ruth and Naomi, and Boaz their kinsman-redeemer (explained further in Chapter 5). They were all remarkable characters and, as we take a closer look at them individually, we will see how each was related to the others and also related to the larger story that God was writing through His people, Israel.

At the beginning of the book of Ruth we meet a woman who needs a redeemer. In these early verses it seems that everyone is suffering and facing adversity. Do you feel that your life is like that too? Do you recognise that you, like Ruth and like every one of us, need a redeemer? Well, Ruth found her redeemer and there is a Redeemer for us too, in this the twenty-first century.

Now we too can belong to a redeemed people. Christians are redeemed. The central theme of redemption in Scripture is that God has taken the initiative to act with the utmost compassion on behalf of those who are powerless to help themselves. Divine redemption includes God's identification with humankind in our plight, securing our liberation through the obedience, suffering, death and resurrection of His incarnate Son. Our Lord Jesus Christ has paid the full price for us by giving His life on the cross for us and for our sins.

Emmanuel, 'God with us', is another name for Jesus. God gave His only Son to the world. He came as a helpless baby. He came in human form that we might see what God is like.

Pastor, writer and international teacher, Rick Howard, defines redemption as coming 'into the fullness of your intended value'. Jesus has paid the full price for us. We are a redeemed people and we can achieve this 'coming into the fullness of our intended value' by being joined to God's redemptive purposes and God's redeemed people. It is the chief way by which our lives become significant. To be redeemed means that we can make a difference in whatever circumstance we find ourselves because we too are part of God's larger story. Christ's atoning sacrificial death on the cross has to be received personally by every Christian believer and, in this way, every individual is caught up in the epic story.

There is a desire in the human heart to be part of something bigger than ourselves. This is what we experience in a small but powerful way, in the natural realm, when we celebrate something of national importance like the Jubilee of Queen Elizabeth or England playing in the World Cup. Millions are united in their common interest and experience a tremendous sense of togetherness – and this is but a faint glimmer of what Christians can experience in the spiritual realm.

One of the saddest things that can happen to Christians is failing to recognise that their personal story is significant and congruent with the story God is telling in His universal epic. Far too many, when presented with the fact that they are part of God's great salvation story, respond with something like this: 'I can't believe that my life has any place in the eternal scheme of things. I am too small and insignificant to have any part in God's cosmic purpose.' Their guilt, fears and inferiority combine to make them feel that a place in God's universal purposes may be right for others but not for them.

The story of Ruth, maybe more than any other biblical story, helps us understand that our lives are chapters in the epic of God's salvation history. Eugene Peterson says, 'Ruth is the instance of a person, uprooted, obscure, alienated, who learned to understand her story as a modest but nevertheless essential part of the vast epic whose plot is designed by God's salvation.' Every detail of every believer's life is part of a universal epic – the story of salvation. Under God, every moment of your life *counts.*

The return

Naomi probably longed to go back to the place of her roots. When she decided to return to Bethlehem, Orpah and Ruth began the journey with her. Naomi pleaded with them to go back to their home. She wished them both to find husbands. However, they both insisted, 'We will go back with you to your people' (1:10). They kissed her and wept loudly as they said this, yet Naomi persisted. She used some extremely valid arguments as to why they should go back:

- The Lord's hand is against me (v.13)
- I am too old to have another husband (v.12)
- Even then, if I have sons, it's too long for you to wait until they reach marriageable age

With this second argument, they both wept again. Then Orpah gave her mother-in-law one last, long emotional kiss and took a fateful decision. She bade Naomi goodbye and returned to her people and her gods. With that she went out of the pages of the Bible and redemptive history. She lost the greatest opportunity of her life. We do not hear of her again. She was so close and yet so far from the kingdom of God.

Many of us are like Orpah. We shed tears at meetings, conferences and even in church; we are moved emotionally. But we don't commit our wills to obedience to the Lord. Tears alone are not enough. Our wills must choose God's way also. There must be no indecision. When life becomes difficult or when the world beckons us, we turn back to our 'gods' – the other people or things that we use as substitutes for trusting God.

Orpah and Ruth were both faced with the same choice: to go with Naomi to a new and strange land or to turn back and stay with their own people in the land of Moab. Orpah drew back while Ruth moved on to a new land and a new future.

Ruth's commitment

The choices Ruth made when she chose to go with Naomi to Bethlehem stand in contrast to the behaviour of the previous era under the judges when everyone did what was right in their own eyes. In committing herself to Naomi, she demonstrates the interconnectedness of our lives with others in community. We all have to make choices. We can repudiate or redeem our relationships.

Ruth had the opportunity to repudiate the relationship with Naomi or to redeem it. She expressed her devotion to Naomi in covenantal form. She didn't say, 'I'll travel with you for as long as it suits, and then move on', but she made a commitment, for better or worse. She said,

> 'Don't urge me to leave you. Where you go I will go, and where you stay I will stay. Your people will be my people and your God my God. Where you die I will die, and there I will be buried. May the LORD deal with me, be it ever so severely, if anything but death separates you and me …' (1:16)

What precious words! I suggest that you memorise them. These are not empty words; each one is full of meaning, backed by a strong desire and determination to keep them. This passage was read by his father at my godson's wedding. It was a moving part of the service, chosen by the couple to express in biblical language the commitment they were making to each other.

Ruth's commitment to Naomi was 'until death us do part'– a threefold commitment, not just for a few years, but for her entire life, including the place of her burial. In those days the place of burial was extremely important. In Genesis 50:24–25 we read that Joseph made his brothers swear to take his bones with them when they left Egypt, for burial in the promised land. This was an amazing commitment that Moses and Joshua fulfilled hundreds of years after the Exodus (Exod. 13:19; Josh. 24:32).

Ruth said, 'I'll stick with you, your people, your God.' Ruth joined herself to Naomi, and so began the great redemptive process. There are people with whom we are stuck in our lives. Mothers-in-law may be some of them! Here Ruth had the opportunity to break from Naomi, but that was not the choice she made.

Naomi shows us how to be a gracious in-law. We know that she loved both her daughters-in-law enough to put their welfare above her own and eventually she even loved Ruth to faith in God.

Family loyalties and commitments become redemptive when we avoid the idolatrous mistake of making them an end in themselves. Rabbi Sachs, in his book *The Politics of Hope*, says that the family is the answer to everything and where the hope of mankind lies. The family is of great importance but we must not make our family an idol in this way. It is only when our lives are connected to God's wider story that relationships can become redemptive. All relationships in the domestic home are set in the wider community. We must ask ourselves what attracted Ruth to Naomi, Naomi's people and her God. Naomi, her husband and her sons (whatever their failings to which Beverley referred earlier) must in some way have given powerful testimony to the faithfulness and love of their God. Naomi experienced the terrible tragedy of losing not only her husband but both her sons also and yet something about her attracted Ruth to stick with her and to want to serve her God.

Faithful relationships

What kind of people do we have to become to attract those close to us to God? How can we become women whom God can use for His redemptive purposes in this troubled world? Think for a moment about the people in your world. What do they think of your commitment to them? How would they rate your faithfulness? Does your loyalty ever waver? With whom are you a friend forever?

What about the relationships that are difficult, tense, fractured, broken? Is there anything you can do to resolve the difficulty, ease the tension, bring about reconciliation? Of course, we are not responsible for, nor can we control, how the other people will react or respond. But we are responsible for our part in all our relationships. The more I talk with women the world over, the more I am convinced that the issue dearest to a woman's heart is relationships. Some relationships are good while others cause so much pain and hurt that the result, in some cases, is bitterness and unforgiveness. I urge you today to tackle any unforgiveness in your life. Do all you can to give your relationships a redemptive quality.

We can forgive because we are forgiven people. Forgiveness is a multi-layered process and going through it, as in dealing with an onion, we may shed tears along the way. It begins with a decision to forgive, responding to the biblical command to do so. If you wait until you *feel* like forgiving, you may never get started. Let me repeat: we *can* forgive because we have been forgiven. When we realise how much God has forgiven us and surrender our will to Him, He supplies the power we need to offer forgiveness to others. I heard Stuart Briscoe say on Premier Radio some time ago that when we forgive we are most like God. How true!

A woman once told me a story involving a neighbour with whom she had extreme difficulties for about a year. The man persisted in putting his rubbish over her boundary onto her land, causing her a great deal of distress and aggravation. She had brought the matter to her church leaders, prayers had been said on her behalf and she committed herself to being forgiving in the situation. When Christmas came and she was writing her cards in her daughter's presence, she felt prompted, to her daughter's astonishment, to send one to this troublesome person. She put it through his door and was amazed when, an hour or so later, one came through her door from him! Her simple act produced a change of heart between them, a spirit of co-operation developed and the difficulties melted away!

Here is another story where I have changed the names in order to share it with you. A woman wrote to me, saying,

> A couple of years ago, when you visited our part of the country, I told you that my daughter had not invited me to her wedding. You were so loving and positive and prayed for me that day, enabling me to continue, with my sadness lifted. I determined to continue to pray and work towards building a relationship with my daughter. Jenny, my daughter, had a little boy called Alun. My father's name was Allen but my daughter did not know this when choosing her son's name. We have seen Alun several times now and this weekend Jenny with her husband Gary invited us up to Worcester to stay. We had a lovely time with them. I felt prompted to write this to you as so often we just don't know the outcome of our prayers.

I have to say that I was extremely moved and encouraged by that letter. What impresses me is the *commitment* she made after we had prayed – 'I determined to continue to pray and work towards building a relationship with my daughter'– and I rejoice with her at the joyful outcome.

We can *all* take part in God's larger redemptive story and relate redemptively to each other because we are linked to God's redemptive love and power.

Let's keep all this in mind as we go on through Ruth's story together.

Questions for reflection

- What questions, relating to your circumstances, are you asking God today?
- How do you see yourself as part of God's great salvation story?
- What kind of person attracts others to God? Be specific about their qualities. Are you such a person?
- What specific changes need to be made for you to become a woman God can use for His redemptive purposes in this troubled world?
- Are there relationships needing to be restored in your life? Is there someone you need to forgive? What, specifically, will you do to begin the process?

Chapter Three

Ruth – Love's Resolve

Jeannette Barwick

'May you be richly rewarded by the LORD, the God of Israel, under whose wings you have come to take refuge.'

(Ruth 2:12)

What amazing courage Ruth displays when she shows her willingness to forsake all that is familiar and sets out with Naomi towards a new country and a new future. Consider also her moving commitment to Naomi. Few people, least of all mothers-in-law, have been promised, let alone been given, such loyalty. She chose to commit herself to Naomi and to her people but, best of all, she decides to put her faith in Naomi's God.

Loving commitment

The Jewish commentator Rabbi Zeira said of the book of Ruth, 'This scroll, there is nothing in it about impurity and purity, about things permitted or not permitted – so why was it written? To teach us how great is the reward for performing deeds of faithful love.' Ruth is wonderfully rewarded for her loving commitment and attention to her mother-in-law. This traditional story, telling of a woman's faithfulness to God and her people, was recorded as an example for later generations to follow. It is read each year at the Jewish Festival of Weeks, the harvest festival. Ruth's story (like Esther's) focuses on faithfulness as the means by which God's purposes for the nation would be fulfilled.

Naomi and Ruth arrived in Bethlehem at the beginning of the barley harvest (1:22) and Ruth had no difficulty in finding gainful employment: at harvest time there was always work to be found in the fields, even if it was only gathering up after the reaping of the harvest. Often, because of the speed at which the reapers worked, small sections would be left unharvested. These would then be covered by gleaners who would walk behind and reap the grain still standing. Jewish law demanded that the gleanings be left for the poor and the alien, and the grain collected by the gleaners became theirs by right (Lev. 19:9–10; Deut. 24:19). During the harvest, all the fields were open for gleaning. No employment agency. No special selection system. No union cards. Those who had the need and desire to glean simply went and worked wherever they wished.

With Naomi's blessing, Ruth took on the role of gleaner. She displayed a beautiful, humble attitude to her mother-in-law and Naomi said, 'Go ahead my daughter.' How close those two had become. It's very special when that happens between daughter-in-law and mother-in-law, or indeed mother-in-law and son-in-law.

I married an only child and from the beginning my mother-in-law, who had miscarried her first child (a girl), was warmly accepting of me. As the years went on we became good friends and, although severely disabled by osteoarthritis, she was always as supportive and helpful as she could possibly be to my husband and me and our two little girls. The breakdown of my marriage caused great sadness all round but my mother-in-law's words to me at the time were, 'Whatever has happened, you'll always be my daughter.' Those words are as precious to me now as when they were spoken.

The providence of God

So Ruth went gleaning and she happened to find herself reaping in one of the fields which belonged to Boaz, who was of the family of Elimelech. The term 'As it turned out' used in 2:3 is filled with deep spiritual meaning. Divine guidance was at work and we see here the unfolding of God's amazing providence. Ruth was being obedient to her commitment. She humbled herself and went out to collect grain as a gleaner. There were probably hundreds of barley fields in Bethlehem and the surrounding area but the Lord guided her into one field in which He could work out His glorious destiny for her life. Ruth probably did not realise it or sense it, for most divine guidance takes place when we are not conscious of it. Eliezer, Abraham's servant, experienced similar leading when he went to search for a bride for Isaac: 'As for me, being on the way, the LORD led me …' (Gen. 24:27, NKJV).

Providence is a word which comes from two Latin words: *pro*, which means 'before', and *video* which means 'to see'. So God, who sees our way before us, says to us today, 'I will guide you with My eye' (Psa. 32:8, NKJV).

Aren't you aware, as you look back over your life, that God guided you when you did not realise it? No flashing lights, no ringing bells, but you were guided nevertheless. Theologians refer to it as 'unconscious guidance'. How thankful we can be that our Master is working for our highest good – even when we are not aware of it. Coincidences become 'God-incidences' as we realise our great God is at work. God never leads us in ways that are contrary to His Word. As we step out in obedience to Him, walk with Him and carry out our commitment to Him, He, our Lord and Master, begins to work out His sovereign will in and through us. And He does it in the most seemingly natural ways. So it was for Ruth and so it is for us.

Through a series of very ordinary incidents, Ruth stumbled into a field where an amazing destiny began to be worked out, with implications for the whole world!

'Whose woman is that?'

So, of all the fields available to her (2:3), Ruth 'happened' to find herself gleaning in one belonging to Boaz, and where he soon arrived. His reception shows that his relationship with his workers was far removed, generally speaking, from those characterising management–labour relations today: Boaz greets them with the words (2:4) 'The Lord be with you!' and the workers reply, 'The Lord bless you!' Can you imagine that kind of exchange of greeting taking place on the factory floors or offices in today's world? Yet when godliness prevails in a nation, one of the first things to be affected is management–labour relations. During the 1904 revival in Wales, many officials in the coalmines met daily with the miners to pray together before the day's work began. This is what an old Welsh miner has to say, 'Dead on the stroke of 6.00am, the manager would appear, followed by other officials of the mine, and greet us with the word "*Bendegedig*" (wonderful). The assembled men would then respond with "Hallelujah", or something similar.' What a way to begin a day!

The secret of good employer–employee relations is for management to be caring, fair minded and honest, and for workers to put in a good day's work. And where there is a Christian commitment on both sides there is added great weight to the qualities I have mentioned.

Boaz makes his way through the field, talking to his workers and then his eye falls upon the figure of Ruth. 'Who is she, whose woman is that?' he asks. His steward tells him that she is the widowed daughter-in-law of Naomi, a Moabitess by birth; that she had requested permission to glean in that field and, taking only a short break, had worked steadily all the time.

She was identified by her country of origin, her relationship with Naomi and by her hard work. We too often draw our identity from these things: we think of ourselves in different ways, such as a wife, a mother, a nurse, a manager, a Methodist, a Baptist. Sometimes, when change occurs, we lose our sense of identity and take a new identity from the circumstance we find ourselves in. This happened to me when, following the failure of my marriage some years ago, I found that I was thinking of *myself* as a failure. Like many in such circumstances, I equated the failure of my marriage with failure as a person. It was God who lovingly showed me that this is not true and, as He lifted my gaze to His, He brought His healing and restoration into my soul. I found my real identity in who I am *in Him* – His own daughter, beloved and precious in His sight – and I allowed His unconditional love to flood my heart.

People need to know they are valued and this was a truth Boaz both believed and practised. He went over to Ruth and said, 'Don't go and glean in another field and don't go away from here … I have told the men not to touch you. And whenever you are thirsty, go and get a drink from the water jars the men have filled' (vv.8–9). Even though Ruth had to work hard, she was thankful for what she had and, receiving such thoughtful care from Boaz, she asked, 'Why have I found such favour in your eyes that you notice me – a foreigner?' (v.10).

'Under whose wings'

Clearly, Boaz already knows of the return of Naomi and how her daughter-in-law Ruth has stayed at her side. The love and devotion of this Gentile girl from Moab must have touched many hearts in Bethlehem. Boaz knows about her but had not met her until that day. He sums up his feelings in the words, 'May the LORD repay you for what you have done. May you be richly rewarded by the LORD, the God of Israel, under whose wings you have come to take refuge' (2:12). Not only did Boaz let Ruth know she was valued but, even more significantly, he expressed the Lord's love and valuation of her. He blessed her on the Lord's behalf.

Ruth discovered God could be her hiding place and she found refuge under His wings. Turning to God in her need was a declaration of faith. She was able to surrender and let herself and her sorrow rest in God, in a relationship of growing intimacy and trust.

What does 'taking refuge' or 'hiding under the wings of the Almighty' actually mean? We all know moments when our world seems to fall apart and everything goes wrong. How do we react when we are hurt and disillusioned? Some of us will try to restore things, cost what it may. Unable to accept what has happened, we may turn bitter and start questioning God. Others, however, may find their faith and their relationship with the Lord deepen in the very 'pit experiences' that bring us down. Some seem to get stuck, whereas others are able to move forward, finding spiritual enrichment in the process of learning to cope with their pain.

Ruth chose the latter way and, hiding in God, she gave evidence of her faith in His goodness and sovereignty, a faith that was stronger than her sorrow. In surrendering to the Lord, her heart found a home, at peace.

So, what does it mean to hide in God? Hiding in God is one of the most difficult, yet one of the most precious things we can experience. It is difficult because, time and time again, we are tempted to think that we can manage on our own. Often, as Beverley honestly confessed in the first chapter, we find it easier to trust ourselves, other people or even circumstances, than to trust God. It is difficult because we are often far removed from the reality of walking with God. Our hurried existence keeps us so occupied with worldly things that we become alienated from heaven. Besides, the childlike trust involved in hiding in our heavenly Father seems to go against everything we know or think we know. Maybe that is why we need to experience moments in life when we are, as it were, laid bare, stripped of our securities, be they people, things or circumstances that are familiar and dear to us. These are the moments when we crave security, comfort and restoration and, too often, turn to other comforters rather than to God.

Some years ago, I was diagnosed with cancer of the colon and needed an operation. I met with the surgeon and a date for the operation was set for just a few days' time. Leaving the consulting room, I drove straight down into the town, went to the big department store and bought myself a handbag. How good an illustration that is of the well-known saying: 'When the going gets tough, the tough go shopping'! There are many things we can turn to in our search for comfort, ranging from alcohol or tranquillisers to romantic novels or food. A friend who is a 'chocoholic' says she doesn't eat chocolate when she is hungry, but when she is lonely, hurt or needing comfort. The point I am making is not that such things are necessarily harmful in themselves but, simply, that they are comforters.

Yet it is our experiences in the very valleys of life that can drive us into the arms of God. There we find that 'pit experiences' can become depth experiences when, hiding in God, we find security, healing and new strength. Under the wings of the Almighty we will know something of God's love which David says is better than life (Psa. 63:3).

God's protection

The image of a bird protecting her young under her wings (2:12) conveys vividly the protection of the Lord (Matt. 23:37; Luke 13:34). We can draw close to Him and experience His protective care and loving concern as we nestle beneath the shelter of His great wings. Those who by faith come under the wings of divine grace may indeed be sure of a rich reward.

Each time I read of Ruth finding refuge under the wings of the Lord, I am moved by the implication of these words. They communicate a wonderful concept that isn't easily grasped at first. Sometimes, certain negative events cause us to lose our trust in people. At times we lose faith even in ourselves. Sometimes, and especially when we feel utterly helpless, our trust in God can be shaken or even lost. Rather than coming closer, we seem to draw back from Him. Hiding in Him, however, communicates the very opposite: a nearness that is difficult to put into words. It is the response to God's unconditional loving welcome. He invites us to take shelter with Him, longing for us to allow Him to enfold and cover us, pain, questions and all!

This was something I experienced personally in a most meaningful way. When my cancer diagnosis became more widely known, my friends at *Woman Alive* magazine sent me their love and prayers along with the verse we are considering, and God used this as a wonderful encouragement as I recovered from surgery. I live overlooking a riverbank and, within days of my diagnosis, a pair of swans chose to nest there, beneath my kitchen window. They became an amazing visual aid to me. That Scripture and the sight of the newly-hatched cygnets nestling under the wings of their parents brought home to me as never before the reality of God's overshadowing presence. I felt calm and relaxed as the truth became a reality to me, reinforced by what was happening day by day, week by week and month by month, under my kitchen window. The faithful care of the swans, first for the eggs, then for the tiny cygnets right through to their full-grown maturity, was one of God's lovely ministrations to me that assisted my healing over the months.

The imagery of taking refuge under God's wings is one of snuggling up to our heavenly Father, looking for warmth and comfort and the safety of 'home'. It involves both trust and trustworthiness, a thought developed by Eleonore (Noor) van Haaften , a Dutch TV producer and broadcaster and a fine Christian speaker and writer, in her book *A Refuge for My Heart*.[1] I am grateful to her for insights I have incorporated into my chapters in this book.

One such insight is that taking refuge in the Lord is perhaps not always a conscious choice: in our state of desperation, it may be the only way, our only hope when there is nothing else left to do. Our search for God often starts in times of trouble and then turns into a process of growth in which our relationship with Him deepens as we learn increasingly to rest in Him.

The importance of acceptance

Noor points to acceptance as an important aspect of finding our hiding place in God. She explains that, when confronted with painful events, one feeling dominates – the longing for things to be reversed and to be the same as, or even better than, they were before tragedy struck. The fact is, she writes, that some things are irrevocable and others can only be partly restored. As we know, there is nothing we can do to alter reality when a loved one dies, or a baby is born with a severe handicap or when, as in my own experience, a family member develops dementia.

When, in her eighties, my own dear mother gradually descended into the confusing world of dementia, I and her whole family longed for the process to be halted and reversed. One day she rang me in tears because she was preparing lunch for herself and my father and she could not remember how to cook the chicken. She, who had cooked for numbers of family and friends over the years and had been responsible for significant catering events at our church, could not remember how to cook two portions of chicken. I comforted her and told her what to do but, as I put the phone down, everything in me screamed out in pain and anger and anguish, wanting to turn back the clock to how she used to be. Of course, that was not possible and peace only came to me as I was able to accept, not fight against, the inevitability of her deteriorating situation. The peace that only God can give transcends our understanding and guards our hearts and minds in Christ Jesus (Phil. 4:7).

Noor points out that, because of its nature, acceptance will rarely be an instant decision but rather the fruit of a gradual process of change in our thoughts and feelings. It is not to be equated with resignation which implies a sense of hopelessness and of something to which we are forced. Because true acceptance is voluntary it is liberating in its effect, whereas forced acceptance contains an element of reluctance and often results in ongoing and painfully strenuous efforts at reversal, and a sense of barely surviving in the situation. There is goodness in facing reality and allowing ourselves time to face our pain and work things through, as best we can, and in this way we become free people.

Naomi and Ruth each had their own unique experience and pain. They also reacted uniquely. Ruth, in hiding in God, found freedom and possessed a quiet assurance in the midst of her own turmoil. She left her worries and grief with the Lord in whom she had found refuge. She was able to stand up straight and go forward with hope. Her zest and courage were stimulating. She was able to carry her mother-in-law along. God remains the same in all circumstances but while some seem to become distanced from God, others seem to be driven to Him. In the story of Ruth and Naomi, we see Him both present and in control. He is never helpless or at a loss even when His children are suffering. Moreover, He is not just *there*, from the beginning to the end, but He is actively present as the One who is in charge of things, controlling, overseeing and giving us courage to move forward.

Ruth found peace and new energy, not just for herself but for others as well. She didn't desert Naomi: in fact, she was a tower of strength and a great comfort to her. The truth is, once you find a hiding place in God, you are in a position to be a blessing to others, even when you are going through a difficult time yourself.

Perhaps some of you, reading this, will be suffering the pain of broken relationships and experiencing feelings of rejection, betrayal or disappointment. You may be in the midst of difficult circumstances due to loneliness, illness, bereavement or some other painful loss. Some have stood firm in their faith despite great criticism from family and friends. God has a special word for you today.

The Almighty has seen all your tears, all your heartache, all your sacrifices, and He promises you a perfect reward one day. Draw close to Him and nestle beneath the shelter of His great wings. Look up and see how easily they cover you. Under His wings there is no further need for tears – just nestle and trust.

Questions for reflection

- Have there been times in your life when you have been aware of God's providence? If so, take time to express your thoughts and feelings about this to God.
- From what do you draw your identity? Is it your role, your work, your family, your relationships? How would you respond if any of these sources of identity were to be threatened or withdrawn?
- What kind of a boss are you? Maybe you are not a boss in paid employment but there are other areas in your life where you have responsibility for others – in the home or in the church maybe.
- In moments when you crave security, comfort and restoration where do you go for satisfaction? Do you hide in work and more work? Do you find comfort in a shopping spree? Do you reach for food, drink, tablets?
- Can you identify 'pit experiences' in your life? How have you responded to them and how, in particular, have they affected your relationship with God?
- How could you begin to be more like Ruth as you face the difficulties God allows in your life?

Note

1. Eleanore (Noor) van Haaften, *A Refuge for My Heart* (Hodder & Stoughton, 1997).

Chapter Four

Handfuls on Purpose

Jeannette Barwick

'And let fall some handfuls for her on purpose and let them lie there for her to glean ...'

(Ruth 2:16, Amp)

Philip Greenslade describes the book of Ruth as the story of 'three funerals and a wedding'! It is a complete narrative in its own right but must not be read in isolation. It is a love story, but not a Mills and Boon one. It tells of two women, Ruth and Naomi, devoted to each other and living out a pure and godly loving relationship. It is clear that Ruth appreciated her mother-in-law and loved her deeply, and that love was expressed in a loyalty that surpassed all other ties. In Naomi Ruth had a mentor and, as we will see, she wisely followed her advice. It is their story that leads us into God's epic story, the larger story of redemption that He is writing for all mankind. And any one of us can get into that story – providing we enter through the door – our Lord Jesus Christ.

The story takes Naomi and Ruth from relative fullness to emptiness, sorrow and loss and once again to fullness. We have seen their arrival in Bethlehem and the favour Ruth has found with Boaz, who provides for both women through Ruth's work in his fields. Boaz, in his knowledge of her and his kindliness to her, removes all her fears and anxieties (2:13). Her faith 'under the wings' of the Almighty has led her into ways of humility. She is content to be a gleaner. She humbly trusts in the graciousness of Boaz.

God's general provision

A thought that needs continually to engage our attention is that when we come empty-handed to God, He fills our hands with blessings that never fail to satisfy and delight our soul. He did this for Ruth and Naomi and He will do this for us too. Jehovah Jireh is God our provider. God has made general provision for mankind through creation. There is enough food on Planet Earth to feed all those who live here. The problems of famine and poverty experienced in the twenty-first century come about not, primarily, through lack of resources, but through man's inhumanity to man, uneven distribution of wealth and unfair trade restrictions.

It is often the case that people who have much want still more, but a different story was told by a couple from one of the more peaceful African countries who came to train on a residential counselling course at Waverley Abbey House, CWR's ministry centre, not long after it was opened. Alice and Bomba told us about their people who had few, if any, material possessions but found fulfilment in their simple lifestyle. As they lived near to the equator, the climate was always warm and the regular rainfall gave rise to four growing seasons a year. Homes were constructed from the natural materials around them. By working the land, people were able to provide themselves with most things for their daily needs. Bomba said his people were largely content with what they had and he and Alice delighted to minister to them, bringing the message of the saving love of Jesus Christ, Son of God the Father, their Creator God, Jehovah Jireh. I found this a salutary tale as one who lives in the developed world where we regard so many of our luxury possessions as necessities! Alice and Bomba trained alongside people from more affluent and sophisticated parts of the world, yet knowing that CWR's Bible-based counselling model for understanding people would be just as effective in their culture as any other. The Word of God touches lives at the deepest level, notwithstanding any barriers cultural differences might present.

God's special provision

Because of His great love for Israel, God had earlier made provision, through the Law, for specific and vulnerable people groups, aliens, the fatherless and widows, not excluding any (Deut. 14:28–29). Thus, built into society, was a level of care and protection for those outside the close family structures that reflected the caring nature of the Godhead. Ruth was a stranger and a foreigner yet the Law made provision for her and she had a right to glean with the Israelites.

On that first day, Boaz continued to ensure that Ruth's work as a gleaner was as free from problems as possible. We mentioned earlier that he told her not to go into any other field but to stay with his own servant girls and to drink from the water jars whenever she was thirsty (2:8–9). His protective concern led him to invite Ruth to join him during a meal break. 'Come over here,' he says. 'Have some bread and dip it in the wine vinegar' (2:14). A little later he offers her some roasted grain. She responds with gratitude and humble obedience. Harvest was a time of much revelry and celebrations and, mindful of her vulnerability, Boaz warned the young men, 'Don't touch her.' She was also told to stay close to his servant girls.

We, too, need to stay close to one another in the Body of Christ. It is not wise to think, 'I don't need anyone. I can manage alone. I don't need a church or fellowship.' There is protection in the fellowship of believers. Above all, there is the security of God's presence and guidance. Boaz also told Ruth, 'Don't glean in another field.' He knew there would be dangers for her in other fields; his fields were fields of grace, others were not. We, too, need to stay within God's grace and faithfulness and not move into other fields. This reminds us of the problem with the Galatian churches where, having been saved by grace, the new believers began to depend on something other than grace for spiritual security. Paul pleads with them, having begun by faith in the grace of God, not to move into legalism, writing,

> You foolish Galatians! Who has bewitched you? Before your very eyes Jesus Christ was clearly portrayed as crucified. I would like to learn just one thing from you: Did you receive the Spirit by observing the law, or by believing what you heard? Are you so foolish? After beginning with the Spirit, are you now trying to attain your goal by human effort?' (Gal. 3:1–3)

Eugene Peterson addressed them in his paraphrased version of the Bible, *The Message*, as 'you crazy Galatians!'

How do you think Ruth felt on that first day of gleaning? She had come to the field that morning a destitute woman and had heard Boaz say, 'I want my Lord to reward you richly. I want you to experience his abundant blessing on your life.' Now he was showing that he himself was eager to be part of the Lord's blessing on her. He poured out his kindness upon Ruth. What comfort this must have brought her in her new sense of security!

Handfuls on purpose – God's generosity

Once Ruth has completed her meal, she returns to her gleaning. Yet again, Boaz intervenes on her behalf, instructing his servants (v.16) to let fall whole handfuls of grain so that she has plenty to gather. I like the way the Amplified Bible describes this moment: 'And let fall some handfuls for her on purpose …' 'Handfuls … on purpose.' What a beautiful expression! We are given a picture of the God who goes before each one of His toiling servants and lets fall 'handfuls on purpose' – some tokens of His goodness, some special encouragement, some evidence of His care, that serves to keep us moving forward with our hearts bent on the divine task.

Make no mistake, the work Ruth was doing was hard work. It was dusty and thirsty work on a hot day. She had to play her part but Boaz, in that safe environment, provided for her abundantly. He provided not just enough to eat and a little grain to take home at the end of the day but more lunch than she could eat and an amount to take home way over and above what she could have hoped for, or dreamed of, at the start of that day. She had a whole ephah of barley (which the Living Bible describes as 35 litres (2:17)) to take home to the eagerly awaiting Naomi.

Boaz shows us the kind of God we have. A God who delights to fill our empty hands again and again, to light our way with evidences of His love, to drop in our path 'handfuls on purpose'.

Sometimes we miss the 'handfuls' that God puts in our way. We stand empty-handed, crying for help, but we have our own ideas about what we need to help us and end our distress and these may prevent us from seeing God's provision. Larry Crabb, the well-known psychologist and biblical counsellor in the USA, tells how, when he was four years old, he locked himself in the bathroom and was unable to get out again. His anxious cries were soon heard by his parents who spoke reassuringly from outside the door. Larry says his gaze never left the door, confident that his parents would be rescuing him through there. Suddenly he heard a sound behind him and his father, who had climbed up a ladder outside, came in through the window to rescue him. Help had indeed come to Larry but from a different and unexpected direction.

How often do we gaze in the wrong direction and miss what God is doing in our lives? We long for a new partner or for physical healing; we wish our loneliness would end, our financial problems be solved or an unpleasant colleague or neighbour transferred. These wishes aren't automatically fulfilled. Yet God is the same faithful One, whether or not the situation changes. He looks at each individual, desiring to bless and to fill empty hands, but sometimes His answer comes from an unexpected angle and takes us by surprise. Sometimes He acts in ways that are not very obvious. We can be so obsessed with the things that are not happening as we wanted and expected that we fail to notice God's blessing.

A woman spoke to me, some time ago, at one of our seminars, her expression heavy with disappointment: someone had prophesied over her life and she had waited in vain for several years for this prophecy to be fulfilled. Her life was clearly empty and purposeless and she was closed to anything else that God might be doing in her life. My heart went out to her but I found it difficult to affirm that prophetic word. Over the years I have heard similar stories from those who have ended up disappointed with God because words, well-intentioned but not inspired by the Holy Spirit, had failed to produce the expected outcome. If something like that happens to you, may I urge you to check it with others, preferably your church leaders, as God will always confirm His word in several ways. We should never speak such 'words' to others glibly, or just out of a desire to encourage, but speak tentatively and always suggest seeking confirmation elsewhere.

Sometimes, it is even possible, because of unbelief or lack of expectation, for us to turn down God's blessing. In 2 Kings 5:1–15, we are told that Naaman, being told by the little slave girl about the miracles of the prophet Elisha, went to Israel to seek healing of his leprosy. Told to bathe seven times in the River Jordan, Naaman at first refused. Surely the Syrian rivers were better than the Jordan? It was his servants who persuaded him to humble himself and obey the prophet's command – and then 'his flesh was restored and became clean like that of a young boy' (2 Kings 5:14).

Openness to God is always an important factor. When we look to Him as the source of our help and consolation, He will find a way of meeting us and bringing us 'handfuls on purpose', even in the most dire of situations. God will make a way and sometimes chooses the most unusual channels.

In an issue of his daily devotional, *Every Day with Jesus*, Selwyn Hughes tells this story:

> Only once in my life have I ever felt deep despair. It happened early in my ministry. The period was such a dark one that I envisaged it would only be a matter of time before I would run out of energy and my ministry would come to an end. Do you

know what turned things around? It was not a verse from the Bible. It was a little bird. While I was sitting in a park feeling thoroughly disillusioned a sparrow hopped on to my hand. How often will a sparrow hop on to someone's hand? It stayed there for several minutes and, as I looked at it, I reflected on what an amazing bird a sparrow is. Through all the seasons of the rolling year he continues with us. Here in Britain you will hear him chirping cheerily amid the snow in dreary December, you will discover him perched on a bare brown twig in the bleakest day in January, you will find him begging on your doorstep when frost has glued the ground in February. Right through the wintry weather he abides. While a swallow darts off to the sun, the sparrow stays at home and braves the stormy blast. The thought came into my mind: 'If he can fight, so can I.' A sparrow sent by God pulled me back from the edge of despair. Emily Dickinson wrote: 'Hope is the thing with feathers, that perches in the soul. And sings the tune without words, and never stops at all.' It's astonishing what God will use to come to our aid when despair overtakes us.

Selwyn received that 'handful' from God. It encouraged his heart and he went on to decades of rich and fulfilling worldwide ministry, including writing *Every Day with Jesus* for more than 40 years.

On a ministry visit to Sri Lanka some years ago, after the main seminar programme in Colombo had concluded, the team went up into the hill country where the tea is grown for a few days' rest. At the Sunday morning service in the small Anglican church, was a Canadian couple with a dozen or so Sri Lankan children. Afterwards we spoke to them. The husband and wife told us that they were responsible for an orphanage that had been founded by the wife's father. Following his death, the home had great financial difficulties. With no money to fund the continuing care of the children, they needed to return to Canada to raise support. They attended the Anglican service as usual on Sunday. As they left the church they encountered a couple from Scotland who 'happened' to have arrived at the wrong time for the service. They took them back to the orphanage for lunch. When the Scottish couple returned to Glasgow, they stayed overnight with an aunt on their way home from the airport. She told them that, having spent some days putting her finances in order, she was somewhat irritated at the arrival of a substantial cheque that she had overlooked. She asked her niece and nephew if they knew of any need to which that money could be put. Unselfishly, they told her about the little orphanage high in the hills in Sri Lanka. Shortly after that, the Canadian couple received that entire sum of money, providing for the children for a whole year and enabling them to return to Canada to make financial provision for the longer-term future. Mark it and mark it well, whatever our circumstances, God *will* meet with us and bless us.

Channels of God's blessing

God's blessing may come to us through special friendships. Undoubtedly, one of the great blessings of Naomi's life was the presence and faithfulness of her daughter-in-law, Ruth. Naomi may not have been aware of the fact that the Lord Himself was reaching out to her through Ruth. She may not have recognised that it was, in fact, much more than simply human support offered to her.

When my marriage broke down, I was heartbroken and in much anguish. I had two friends, Joy and Cecilia, who particularly ministered to me. Others were a great help as well, but these two seemed especially sensitive, knowing just when to phone or call round, when to speak or when to be silent but comforting companions. I thank my God for every remembrance of them; their friendship to me in those days was indeed 'as from the Lord'.

Sometimes, on our life's journey, when we are blinded by bitterness or pain, God, by His grace, gives us people as special comforters who become visual aids reflecting to us the very concern of God Himself. Often the best comforters are those who have suffered themselves but have found a refuge for their hearts in the God of all comfort. Ruth was like that: she carried her own load of sorrow and yet, somehow, she had sufficient strength to be a source of support and comfort to her mother-in-law. Naomi had a comforting and wonderful companion in Ruth. That is, in fact, one of the ways in which the Lord filled her empty hands again. Friendship is a great and precious gift. We need to develop an eye for it and come to appreciate more of what is given to us in our friends.

Then again, there is the blessing of intercessory prayer. One very special area in which friends can deeply bless one another is that of prayer. When someone is feeling overwhelmed by her life circumstances, friends can lift her to God's throne of grace in intercessory prayer. We can do that for others, others can do that for us and, in so doing, we mobilise 'the things of God' that surpass even the best we can humanly give one another. During my weeks of post-operative recovery and chemotherapy, I was aware of the prayers of many around the world that were a tremendous source of strength and comfort to me. I felt as though God accelerated all the healing processes in my body, mind and spirit in a wonderful way. He used that experience not just to restore me to physical health but to touch every other area of my life as well.

Naomi must have waited impatiently for Ruth to return at the end of that first day. As soon as she sees Ruth laden with all those provisions, she plies her with questions (2:19). Where? Who? How? When she hears that Ruth has gleaned in the field of Boaz Naomi's heart leaps within her and she begins to focus on the Lord possibly as she has never quite done before. 'The LORD bless him!' she says of Boaz; '[the LORD] has not stopped showing his kindness to the living and the dead' (2:20). Her joy knows no bounds because she senses that Ruth's meeting with Boaz has a providential feel about it. She knows that Boaz, as a close relative, has the right to redeem Ruth and take her to be his wife.

Together, Ruth and Naomi would have looked back over the day and given thanks to God for the evidence of His guiding hand. They found, as we have so often found, that the evidences of the divine design are certainly there as we look back. God's abundant provision had been there for them. Boaz said to Ruth (2:21), 'Stay with my workers until they finish harvesting all my grain' and Ruth worked for three long months as a gleaner, bending low in Israel's heat.

As with Ruth and Naomi, each of us can recognise that in the ebb and flow of life's circumstances, our eternal God is quietly pursuing His purposes. Little, if anything, happens by chance in the God-ordained life. The Almighty is seeking to work out His purposes in the life of each one of us and He is there in every situation or emergency that arises.

The thought that, in the life of every one of His children, God is bent on bringing to pass His perfect purposes may not entirely eliminate anxiety and fear, but it most certainly reduces it. All things really do work together for good for those who love the Lord (Rom. 8:28). Many things appear irretrievable to us but there is nothing irretrievable with God. God is working all the time in your life to bring about the purposes of His larger story.

Our hands are filled over and over again by God, in His way and in His time. We must never forget that we follow an almighty and all-powerful God. He is in total control and will never let go of us. Rather, He travels before and with us as a faithful guide and friend, filling our empty hands with His loving kindness, blessing and grace.

These are facts, and facts that can give us confidence and a deep sense of security.

> 'So those who planted their crops in despair will shout hurrahs at the harvest. So those who went off with heavy hearts will come home laughing, with armloads of blessing.'
>
> (Psa. 126:5–6, *The Message*)

Questions for reflection

- What is your general attitude to God's provision in your life? Are you contented or seeking more? If the latter, is it more of God you are seeking or more of something else? Try to be honest with yourself.
- Has there been a time in your life when, overcome with the weight and burden of the day, you were about ready to give up on the task God had given you, and then suddenly He let fall some 'handful on purpose'? Have you experienced such a moment of divine encouragement? Perhaps it was a word in a sermon, a word from Scripture that was quickened by the Spirit to your heart, or perhaps a line in a devotional commentary. Make a note of any such moments and thank God for His loving and gracious provision.
- How might you be failing to find the 'handfuls' God is letting fall in your path? Are there some pre-conceived ideas you might need to let go of in order to open yourself to God's blessing? Identify them and ask God to help you be more receptive.
- Are you enjoying the security to be found only in God's fields? In

what other, possibly dangerous fields, might you be wandering or tempted to wander?

- Think of the friendships in your life. What kind of friend are you? What do you appreciate in your friends? Who might you need to thank, or pray for?
- How might you serve as a channel of God's blessing to others? Think of some specific actions you might take, however small and insignificant they might seem.

Chapter Five

Hand in Hand – God's Hand and Ours

Beverley Shepherd
Original talks given by Beth Clark

'[The LORD] has not stopped showing his kindness to the living and the dead.'

(Ruth 2:20)

The book of Ruth shows us a wonderful interplay of divine sovereignty and human responsibility. God's amazing sovereignty in our lives means that no plan of His can be thwarted.

God's hand

It is Naomi who constantly alerts us to God's hand at work in this story. 'When … the LORD had come to the aid of his people by providing food for them …' (1:6); 'May the LORD show kindness … May the LORD grant … another husband' (1:8–9); '… the LORD's hand has gone out against me!' (1:13); 'The LORD has afflicted me; the Almighty has brought misfortune upon me' (1:21). And now, at the end of chapter 2, she again sees the Lord's hand at work in the 'coincidence' of Ruth working in Boaz's field and Boaz taking notice of her. '[The LORD] has not stopped showing his kindness to the living and the dead' she declares in 2:20.

What should be our response to God's sovereignty – passive acceptance and fatalism? No! God calls us to work hand in hand with Him to bring about His purposes.

Naomi's hand

As Naomi's eyes are opened to what the Lord is doing in Ruth and Boaz's lives, she decides it is now time for her to do her part! There is always a danger when we talk of human responsibility that we will go ahead of God – Naomi waits to see what God is doing before she makes her move.

Naomi would have been aware of God's provision of 'levirate' marriage (coming from the Latin word meaning 'brother-in-law'). This required the brother-in-law to marry the widow of his deceased brother if no heir had been born. The widow was not to remarry outside the family; the brother was then to raise an heir for his dead brother so that his brother's name might be perpetuated and the family inheritance secured (see Deut. 25:5–10). Although Boaz is not Ruth's brother-in-law, he is one of her nearest male kin, and she does therefore have some claim on him to fulfil this duty to her dead husband. Naomi is also aware of her own responsibility, as Ruth's nearest relative, to arrange a good marriage for her.

Notice these helpful principles for action: (1) Observe what God is doing through the circumstances of your life. (2) Is the action required of you in line with God's law? And (3) what are your responsibilities in this situation? God has called us to be partners in working out His plans!

Ruth's hand

Yet Naomi is not the only one with a part to play. She outlines her audacious plan to Ruth. Ruth's total trust in Naomi is breathtaking – not only did we see the abandonment of all she had known and loved to follow Naomi and Naomi's God, now we see her trusting implicitly in Naomi's decision to set up a very unusual meeting between her and Boaz. She was to dress as a bride (washed and perfumed) and not as a servant girl and then to go to the threshing floor where men, having had a good meal and plenty of wine, would be sleeping. She is gambling her reputation and her chastity on the godly character of Boaz and on Naomi's discernment of what God is doing.

I imagine that she didn't sleep a wink, wondering if Boaz would wake, and needing to be ready if he did. Naomi had said that Boaz will know what to do, but Ruth, with godly boldness, asks him to marry her. The term 'spread the corner of your garment over me' is a request for marriage, but there is also a wonderful play on words here – the same words mean 'cover me with your protective wings'. In Ruth 2:12 Boaz prays for Ruth saying: 'May you be richly rewarded by the LORD, the God of Israel, under whose wings you have come to take refuge.' Boaz is to be the answer to his own prayer! God's protection of Ruth is going to happen through Boaz spreading his garment over her and marrying her. Her rich reward is going to be the family life they will enjoy together.

The hand of prior commitment

How many of us would like to start all over again – to be given a blank sheet on which to design the future? When we become Christians our past is washed clean, but it still stands. We still have the same upbringing, family background and commitments – Paul even encourages us in this: 'Each one should remain in the situation which he was in when God called him' (1 Cor. 7:20). Paul particularly applies this to our relational commitments, eg marriage. When Ruth goes to the threshing floor she does so as someone who is totally committed to Naomi. While they were still in Moab, Naomi gave her daughters-in-law the choice to go back to their mothers' homes. They were released from all obligations to her and to their dead husbands. Orpah took this freedom, but Ruth made a covenantal vow and committed herself to stay with Naomi until death. This commitment meant that Ruth was no longer free to 'run after the younger men'. These younger men might have been all too pleased to have Ruth as their wife, but to accept her mother-in-law as part of the package was unlikely. Hence Ruth was obligated to either remain single or to marry a man who would accept that Ruth and Naomi were a package deal, someone who would take Naomi into his house and care for her as well as for Ruth. When Boaz says 'This kindness is greater than that which you showed earlier …' (3:10) he is not depreciating himself as a husband, he is recognising her kindness to Naomi. He knows that he is perhaps the only man who will accept this package deal and who shares Ruth's sense of family responsibility.

You and I have a prior commitment – we were bought with a

price, the price of Christ's death on the cross. We have renounced the choice of returning to our mother's house and have covenanted ourselves to be His through life and into death. This choice means we are not free to bind ourselves to anyone who will not accept that we are a 'package deal' with God. If this seems a hard sacrifice then look again at Ruth – her example shows that God is no woman's debtor.

Yet her commitment to Naomi is not Ruth's only prior commitment – she is committed to Naomi's God as well. This commitment is also recognised by Boaz who says: 'All my fellow townsmen know that you are a woman of noble character' (3:11). The word *hayil*, translated as 'noble', is a word denoting worth. It is also used of the woman in Proverbs 31 – a capable woman (*hayil* implies ability and efficiency) and a woman of moral worth. The word is most often used in the Old Testament of God – the helper of His people. This is not a weak woman, but one who can laugh at the days to come because of her fear of the Lord and total trust in Him. Although Ruth was probably physically attractive, the main reason that Boaz plans such a careful strategy, as we will see, to secure Ruth as his wife is that she is a woman of noble character – a wife worth having!

Having spent the night on the threshing floor at Boaz's suggestion and for her own protection, she returns to Naomi. You can imagine the scene – Naomi, probably having been up all night waiting, is listening for the first sound of Ruth's return. And then here Ruth is, carrying six measures of barley – and Naomi's first words: 'How did it go ...?' – in the Hebrew literally 'Who are you, my daughter?' Naomi wants to know if she is now the prospective Mrs Boaz! Ruth describes all that happened and then wise Naomi's advice is to wait. Again the Hebrew is instructive here as the word Naomi uses has at its root the verb 'to sit'. Sit and wait and trust that Boaz will settle the matter. They have both done their part, now the initiative passes to Boaz.

Boaz's hand

To be a kinsman-redeemer to Naomi and Ruth involved personal sacrifice – the obligation to provide for both Naomi and Ruth during their lifetimes. The more distant a relative you were, the more voluntary it was to take on the responsibilities of this redemption role. The author makes it increasingly clear that any action on Boaz's part is not dictated by the requirements of the Law – it is dependent on his willingness and generosity. Ruth and Naomi's nearest relative is willing to redeem their property but, by a masterly strategy, Boaz links the role of kinsman-redeemer with that of levirate marriage – the responsibility to father an heir for Elimelech's property through Ruth. This could lead to future family disputes and endanger a man's estate. The cost was too high for the first kinsman-redeemer and he withdraws his claim in the accepted way – by removing his sandal and giving it to Boaz. Boaz, however, is prepared to pay this cost – he understands sacrificial commitment and accepts its price.

We also have a kinsman-redeemer – Jesus Christ. He willingly paid the price to buy us back from slavery to sin, and make us a part of His family. The price was His death on the cross: 'In him we have redemption through his blood, the forgiveness of sins …' (Eph. 1:7). Jesus' act of sacrificial love was voluntary and through it He secured a bride for Himself – the Church. This is why Paul writes: 'Husbands, love your wives, just as Christ loved the church and gave himself up for her …' (Eph. 5:25). It is because we have been redeemed at such a cost that we have an obligation to live redeemed lives, and not as if we were still enslaved to sin. The love story between Ruth and Boaz, wonderful though it is, is merely a pale reflection of the greater love story – that of God and His Church. We are women who know what it means to have been loved sacrificially!

The community's hand

A wedding is not a private affair. Family life is the basis for community life. This was totally understood in Old Testament times and so we see a community response and responsibility to Ruth and Boaz – they pray blessing on them. Throughout the Bible we see the power of blessing: Isaac and his blessing of Jacob, Jacob's prophetic blessing of each of his sons. We should not be surprised at the power of blessing for we are inheritors of the Abrahamic covenant (Gen. 12:1–3) where God declares that He will bless us and we will be a blessing to the whole world. The elders pray a wonderful blessing on Ruth and Boaz – a blessing that includes their reputation and their family life. This is fulfilled through the birth of Obed. Ruth and Boaz are not just ancestors of King David but also of King Jesus! Through their union they are a channel of blessing to the whole world, fulfilling Genesis 12. The women recognise the great blessing Ruth is to Naomi. Naomi who was poor, bereft of family, embittered and empty now is secure in the home of Boaz, her life renewed and her lap full with her precious grandson.

God's hand and ours

It is all too easy to read the story of Naomi, Ruth and Boaz, be warmed by its happy ending and fail to apply its lessons to our own lives. We experience this same tension between divine sovereignty and human responsibility; how are we to live out this tension? The story of Ruth gives us some key principles for doing so: perspective; positioned; perceptive; protected; prepared; and patient.

1. Perspective

Key to living hand in hand with God is having the right perspective on who God is. We need a big picture of Him. For many of us, our

God is too small and although we give lip service to His power, His loving-kindness towards us, His provision and His goodness, we fail to live our lives in a way that evidences these truths. Naomi knows that He is the Almighty whose hand directs her future. Personally, I find it all too easy to say that I trust God in a particular situation, but then to take charge and try to work things out for myself. Spending time in God's Word is key to understanding who God really is. As Psalm 99:1–2 declares:

> The LORD reigns,
>   let the nations tremble;
> he sits enthroned between the cherubim,
>   let the earth shake.
> Great is the LORD in Zion;
>   he is exalted over all the nations.
> Let them praise your great and awesome name –
>   he is holy.

2. Positioned

Are we in the right place to receive God's guidance and provision? It was as Naomi turned away from Moab ('nothingness') and returned to Bethlehem ('House of Bread') that she experienced that '[The LORD] has not stopped showing his kindness to the living and the dead' (2:20). I am not referring to geographic position, for we know that '… if I settle on the far side of the sea, even there your hand will guide me …' (Psa. 139:9–10), but to being in the place of obedience. God guides us one step at a time; He provides a lamp for our feet and not a floodlight into the future. So when we fail to be obedient to the step He is asking us to take, then we are not in the right place to hear the next step from Him. It was only when Naomi retraced her steps back to Bethlehem that she was in a position to discern God's leading regarding Ruth and Boaz. It may be that you and I need to repent of times when we have wilfully disobeyed God's guidance to move in a certain direction or to stay put where we are – only then will we be in the right position to hear His guidance for the future.

3. Perceptive

How is it that Naomi can dare to suggest to Ruth that she should go to the threshing floor at night, risking her reputation and chastity? It can only be because Naomi has been given insight into what God is doing in this situation. I suspect that Naomi has been forced, through circumstances, to become still – since her menfolk have died she has no one at home to look after, no meals to prepare until Ruth returns with grain, no household to organise and no grandchildren to care for. Psalm 46:10 instructs us to 'Be still, and know that I am God …'. As a natural activist, I can find it hard to become still – my mind is racing ahead to all the things that need doing. I need to hear, with Martha, Jesus' loving rebuke: '… you are worried and upset about many things, but only one thing is needed' (Luke 10:41). That one thing is to be still, like Mary, at the feet of Jesus and to listen – only then will we become perceptive as to how God is working in our lives and in the lives of those we love. Let me encourage you not to wait until stillness is forced upon you by circumstances or illness, but to choose to still your heart and listen.

4. Prepared

Before going down to the threshing floor Ruth washes, perfumes herself and puts on her best clothes – she prepares herself to receive God's provision of a husband. So often we petition God in prayer for something and then are caught by surprise when He answers. I love the account in Acts 12 of Peter's miraculous escape from prison. In verse 5 we are told that the church was earnestly praying to God for

Peter, yet when Peter escapes, turns up at the prayer meeting in verse 13 and is announced by the servant girl, they tell her that she must be out of her mind! Thankfully Peter kept knocking and they eventually let him in. How many times I wonder has God's answer to our prayers come knocking at our doors and we haven't let it in? God will give us the wisdom to know how to prepare if we ask Him. As we prepare, we are opening up our hearts and our lives to welcome God's answer – we are creating the space in which to receive His provision.

5. Protected

Walking the streets of Bethlehem at night and then laying down on the threshing floor puts Ruth in a position of extreme vulnerability. Ruth is not doing this on her own initiative – she is directed by Naomi who has been 'watching' what God is doing. Sometimes the step God shows us to take will not feel 'safe', yet, if we seek the wisdom of godly Christians and follow God's leading there is no safer place than in the centre of His will. No loving mother-in-law would then have gone to bed and slept soundly knowing that Ruth was walking the dark streets; she would have been praying for Ruth every minute she was gone. Learn to ask others to pray for you and for your protection as you follow God's leading; and be willing to intercede for them.

6. Patience

Waiting for God's answer can be the hardest part. In Ruth 3:18 Naomi tells Ruth to wait – they have done their part and the initiative now passes to Boaz. We don't know what was going through Ruth's mind, but I suspect that the degree of peace she experienced would have totally depended on how much she trusted both Boaz's commitment to her and his character. The same is true of us. When we place something in the Lord's hands, having done all that He requires of us in prayer or action, then we can peacefully rest and prepare to receive His answer. Why? Because we know that He is committed to us in covenant love – a commitment that led Him to die on the cross for us; and that His Word is trustworthy. Too often my prayers are of the 'delegation' variety, eg, 'Lord, I'm placing this in Your hands, but if you haven't got it done by this time next week, then I'll do it myself!' God will not be delegated to – He is Lord and we are His servants. When we hand a person or a situation over to Him, we do so knowing that He is free to do what He chooses and when He chooses and our role is to wait and to trust.

Learning to live hand in hand with God is exciting! How do we place our hand in His? Through covenantal commitment. Just as, in former times, a man would ask for a woman's *hand* in marriage, so God asks for our hand and awaits our 'Yes!' In the next chapter we explore the richness of covenant.

Questions for reflection

- How big is your God?
- How is this evidenced in your life/lifestyle?
- Is there any area of your life in which you need to 'return from Moab'?
- Allow yourself to become still and reflect on what God is doing in your life.
- What preparation is needed for you to move forward with God?
- Who prays for you regularly? And for whom do you pray?
- Read Psalm 18 and again reflect on 'How big is your God?'

Chapter Six

Covenantal Love

Beverley Shepherd

Original talks given by Beth Clark

'Where you go I will go, and where you stay I will stay.
Your people will be my people and your God my God.'

(Ruth 1:16)

Recently I had the joy of going to two weddings – both couples were dear friends and so both days were very special. On each occasion, two people who loved each other committed themselves to marriage, but there was a difference. The first took place in a registry office where the terminology of 'contract' was used; the second took place in a church where a covenant was made between the husband and wife. On the surface there may seem to be little difference, yet deep down the distinctives of covenant are significant:

- Covenants are based on vows or promises.
- There are no get-out clauses – literally it is 'for better or worse.'
- It is a binding together of the two parties (the root of the word covenant means 'to bind'). Hence, once joined, it cannot be 'put asunder'.
- It can only be ended by death: 'till death do us part.'
- It is made in the sight of God and according to His holy Law – God's Law governs covenant and not the law of the land.
- Faithfulness is key: 'be faithful to her/him as long as you both shall live'. The Hebrew word for faithfulness is *hesed*, translated as kindness or loving-kindness in the book of Ruth.
- It defines lifelong belonging: 'I am yours and you are mine.'

Without an understanding of covenant we cannot fully understand the book of Ruth, for covenantal love is its very heartbeat. Our God is a covenant God – He never enters into permanent relationship except through covenant, so if we want a committed relationship with God we have to embrace covenant. This is the way we put our hand in His. The word 'testament' means covenant and throughout the Old Testament God cuts several covenants with individuals and with His people. He made covenants with Noah (Gen. 6:18; 9:8–17), Abraham (Gen. 15; 17), Moses (Exod. 24) and with David (2 Sam. 7). These covenants contain both promises and responsibilities or obligations.

When God makes a covenant He signs it with His covenantal name: Yahweh (LORD) – the name He gave to Moses in Exodus 3. It is significant that of the 21 times God is named in the four chapters of Ruth, 18 of them use His covenantal name 'LORD'. So let us revisit the book of Ruth through the eyes of covenant.

We learned in Chapter One that 'in the days when the judges ruled' the people of God were indistinguishable from the nations around them. They were inheritors of the Sinai covenant made with Moses and yet they ignored God and treated the Ten Commandments with distain. Although written to reflect a later time in Israel's history, the words of Hosea 4:1–3 give an accurate description of this period as well:

> Hear the word of the LORD, you Israelites,
> because the LORD has a charge to bring
> against you who live in the land:
> 'There is no faithfulness, no love,
> no acknowledgement of God in the land.
> There is only cursing, lying and murder,
> stealing and adultery;
> they break all bounds,
> and bloodshed follows bloodshed.
> Because of this the land mourns,
> and all who live in it waste away …'

We should not be surprised that Bethlehem was experiencing famine when Hosea tells us that the land will mourn when God's people ignore Him and there is no covenantal love and faithfulness in the land.

Into this setting comes Ruth, who shows more understanding of covenant love in her little finger than most Israelites were showing in their whole bodies! Almost her first recorded words in this book take the form of a covenantal commitment:

> But Ruth replied, 'Don't urge me to leave you or to turn back from you. Where you go I will go, and where you stay I will stay. Your people will be my people and your God my God. Where you die I will die, and there I will be buried. May the LORD deal with me, be it ever so severely, if anything but death separates you and me.'
>
> (1:16–17)

These are the words on which the whole book of Ruth turns! The rest of the book is the story of what God can do if we are committed in covenant faithfulness to Him and His people. Through this statement Ruth joins herself to the covenant people of God and becomes an inheritor of the promises made to Noah, Abraham and Moses. As Boaz puts it in Ruth 2:12: 'May you be richly rewarded by the LORD … under whose wings you have come to take refuge.'

In a covenant both parties have obligations to the other. These are expressed in terms of vows or promises. When we make a covenantal commitment to God, He promises us *provision*, *protection* and a *place* in His *purposes*. Our part is well expressed by the vow that Ruth makes to Naomi: to go or stay according to God's leading; to be committed to His people; and to make the Lord our God.

God's promises to His people

Provision

In Chapter Three we explored God's wonderful provision for both Ruth and Naomi. We saw how this included both general provision according to His Law – for example the right given to widows and foreigners to glean – and then the specific provision given to Ruth which goes beyond the requirements of the Law. This is shown in Boaz's provision of water (2:9), bread and wine vinegar (2:14), extra grain (2:16) and six measures of barley (3:15). Similarly the Law allows for the provision of a husband through levirate marriage, yet God's specific provision for Ruth is a man of the character of Boaz who understands covenantal commitment.

Notice that although God may on occasion override human agencies, God's most usual way of providing for us is through His people and through work. God and Boaz had provided the grain in the field – Ruth had to go and pick it up!

God's provision is emphasised in many other passages in the Bible, for example Matthew 6:25–34. In verses 31–33 we are told:

> So do not worry, saying, 'What shall we eat?' or 'What shall we drink?' or 'What shall we wear?' For the pagans run after all these things, and your heavenly Father knows that you need them. But seek first his kingdom and his righteousness, and all these things will be given to you as well.

It is as Ruth sought God's kingdom by committing herself to Naomi, to Naomi's God and to His people, that she experiences the truth that 'all these things will be given to you as well'.

Thankfully I have never had to worry where my next meal is coming from, although I have known times when the budget has been extremely tight. As someone who is self-employed I can be tempted to worry when the work diary looks a bit sparse and I need to remind myself that God is my provider, not any one contract or customer. A significant move forward in this came for me when, for a period of months, I used an expanded version of the Lord's Prayer in my Quiet

Time. The daily repetition of 'Give us today our daily bread' and then thankfulness that God had provided in the past and would provide that day and in the future, planted trust deep into my mind and heart.

If we can trust God to be our provider, why is it that Naomi – a covenant woman – says in Ruth 1:21 that she is empty? I believe that we can experience emptiness when we look for God's provision in the wrong places. Just as Elimelech and Naomi had looked for food in Moab instead of Bethlehem, so we can seek to fill our physical, spiritual or emotional emptiness from sources other than those that God has provided. These sources may satisfy us for a while, but eventually we will be left feeling more empty and desolate than before. It is only when Naomi returns to Bethlehem that she receives God's filling – a grandson on her lap!

Protection

As women on their own, both Naomi and Ruth were extremely vulnerable – in Israelite society protection or 'covering' came from the men in your family. However, for them and for us, the ultimate source of our protection is God. As Psalm 91:1–2 emphasises: 'He who dwells in the shelter of the Most High will rest in the shadow of the Almighty. I will say of the LORD, "He is my refuge and my fortress, my God, in whom I trust."'

A few years ago I travelled round China with my 'little' brother, Blair. Blair is six foot six with broad shoulders developed through years of competitive rowing. Among the short Chinese men he was definitely the 'most high'. It felt so safe being 'in his shadow'. Our God is the Most High – our refuge and our fortress. I have learned to seek His protection not just when there is the potential for physical danger but also when I am in situations of emotional or spiritual danger: protection from the sharp or hurtful words of others; protection from inappropriate relationships; and protection from myself and my tendency to act or speak before I think!

Ruth experiences God's protection throughout this story: she and Naomi are protected on their journey back to Bethlehem; Ruth 'coincidentally' finds herself gleaning in Boaz's field and we learn that in another field she may have been harmed; Boaz is aware that the streets are not safe at night for a woman on her own and so asks her to lie on the threshing floor until morning; he also protects her reputation by saying 'Don't let it be known that a woman came to the threshing floor'.

God's protection does not mean that we are to be oblivious to danger. The very reason that Boaz and the men are sleeping on the threshing floor is that the grain, once threshed, is tempting to robbers. Wise precautions are our responsibility – ultimate protection is God's.

A place in God's purposes

The story of Ruth and Naomi shows us how women, committed in covenant faithfulness to God, find that they have a place in God's salvation purposes for this world. If you have ever been tempted to doubt that your life can be used by God for His purposes, then let the story of these two women encourage you.

Look at Naomi: when we first meet her, her life reflects her name – pleasant: she is married with two sons. Then, due in all probability to the poor decision-making of her husband, she goes to live in Moab – 'exiled' from her home, her people and her religion. She loses her husband, her sons, her role in society, her financial security and her hope. Can God use this empty sorrowing woman? Yes!

It is from Naomi that Ruth learns about the one true God and is so convinced by the example of Naomi's life that this God is worth following, she is prepared to abandon her home to follow Naomi back to Bethlehem. It is Naomi who brings Ruth to Bethlehem and into the salvation purposes of God. It is Naomi that sees God's hand at work in the meeting of Ruth and Boaz and advises Ruth to go to the threshing floor. And ultimately it is Naomi who is given the care of Obed, King David's grandfather.

Look at Ruth: she is brought up in Moab, taught to worship Chemosh and, as a Moabitess, excluded by God's command from Israel (Deut. 23:3–6). A widow, without any close male relatives, she, like Naomi, is destitute.

Yet, at the point that she commits herself in covenant love to Naomi and to Naomi's God, and sacrificially leaves her home and family, she places herself under God's provision and protection and within His purposes. Ruth 'shines like a star' in a crooked and depraved generation (Phil. 2:15). Her committed love for Naomi stands in sharp contrast to the faithlessness and depravity of the people of Bethlehem – so much so that Boaz and all his fellow townsmen knew her to be a woman of noble character. Through her marriage to Boaz and the birth of Obed, Ruth 'the foreigner' is placed in the ancestral line of King David and King Jesus (see Matt. 1:5–16). Through Ruth's son and supremely God's Son the Word of life is held out to this world.

At the point that you and I commit ourselves in covenant love to Jesus and declare Him Lord of our lives, we not only put ourselves under His protective wings and know His provision – our lives have meaning and purpose. In the days when the judges ruled, how was God to carry out His salvation purposes for Israel and for the world? Was it to be through the daring exploits of Samson, the fleeces of Gideon or the wise counsel of Deborah? No, though all of these had their place. Surprisingly God's purposes are carried forward by a poor Moabite widow who pledged herself to the Lord and His people – yes, through Ruth!

Our promises

How are we to respond when God 'asks for our hand' in covenantal commitment to Him? The words of Ruth's promise to Naomi give us an excellent framework:

> Where you go I will go.
> Where you stay I will stay.
> Your people will be my people.
> Your God will be my God.

Where you go I will go

The decision to commit ourselves to Christ is ultimately a decision to become a follower. Jesus' invitation to the first disciples 'Come follow me' still stands. Becoming a Christian is not about making Christ Lord – He is Lord already; it is about Him making us His disciples or followers. *The New Bible Dictionary* (IVP) defines a disciple as the pupil of a teacher. Becoming a disciple of Jesus was initiated by His call, as in Mark 1:16–20 where He calls Simon and Andrew with the words: 'Come follow me and I will make you fishers of men.' Discipleship involved personal allegiance to Him, expressed in following Him and giving Him exclusive loyalty. In every case readiness to put the claims of Jesus first, whatever the cost, was demanded. Such an attitude went beyond the normal teacher–pupil relationship and gave the word 'disciple' a new meaning. It was whole-life discipleship.

Following His leading may take us, like Ruth, away from our friends, family, country and all that is known and familiar. It may seem to jeopardise our best human hopes for marriage as leaving Moab did for Ruth. Yet God is no woman's debtor. Jesus said 'I tell you the truth … everyone who has left houses or brothers or sisters or father or mother or children or fields for my sake will receive a hundred times as much and will inherit eternal life' (Matt. 19:28–29).

How do we follow? The words of the old hymn by John Henry Sammis put it well: 'Trust and obey, for there's no other way.' Obedience implies listening – we cannot obey if we are deaf to God or avoid communicating with Him at all! As with any relationship this means giving time to the other person – time to listen (through Bible study and devotional reading, through prayer and meditation, and through a growing sensitivity to His Holy Spirit's leading). To obey requires trust – especially when the path seems unclear or dangerous. Often it is only as we have moved forward in trusting obedience that we can see that God's plan was for our good.

Where you stay, I will stay

Sometimes staying is harder than going! It carries with it none of the glamour or excitement of the journey. Yet, by staying, we might be the one that enables others to go.

Some years ago I participated in a personal growth course called 'The Challenge of Excellence'. The eight delegates on the course were posed with a variety of physical challenges involving, ropes, walls, water pits, etc. We were given an objective and a time limit and then left to work out, as a team, how we were going to achieve the goal. One exercise involved trying to get as many of us as possible over a 12-foot wall, without the aid of ropes. We eventually found a way of climbing up on each others' shoulders but realised that one person would be left behind – the bottom rung in our human ladder. One woman volunteered. The seven of us that got over the wall by climbing on her shoulders would never have been able to do so without her sacrificial willingness to stay behind.

Your people will be my people

When we become a follower of Christ we are incorporated into His

Body – the Church. God never intended for us to be on our own. One of the key ways in which we demonstrate our commitment to God's people is through 'loving-kindness' – a phrase that is used many times throughout the book of Ruth. This implies kindness in attitude, in words and in actions.

Often it is our words and actions that reflect our attitude. When Boaz approaches Ruth in 2:8 he encourages her to go and drink from the water jars whenever she is thirsty, yet he does more that this, he also speaks to her thirst for kindness. Ruth's most common descriptor in this book is 'the Moabitess' – she is the foreigner, with no friends or family except Naomi. She has voluntarily chosen to leave all that is familiar behind and commit herself to Naomi and Naomi's God. Yet this is not without cost. In a society where most relationships were formed through family connections she only has Naomi, who is herself bereft of close family, as her companion. Ruth's response to Boaz's concern and kindness show that this was water on dry ground. His words also indicate that her sacrifice has not gone unnoticed – by Boaz or God.

Words have incredible power to both hurt us and to heal and encourage us. Paul emphasises this in his letter to the Ephesians when he writes: 'Do not let any unwholesome talk come out of your mouths, but only what is helpful for building others up according to their needs, that it may benefit those who listen' (Eph. 4:29). We have a choice how we use our words. We can use them to criticise, slander, wound, discourage and isolate others. Many of you know what it is like to be on the receiving end of this. Or we can use them as Boaz did, to befriend the lonely, to protect the vulnerable, to recognise godly sacrifice and to pray blessing on God's people – who are now 'my people'.

Your God will be my God

As when a woman marries she is given her husband's surname, so we take the name of our God when we become Christians (literally 'little Christs'). To be given someone's name is to be identified with them – this is both a privilege and a responsibility. We are to reflect the very character of Christ. Is it any wonder that Boaz, who exemplified covenant faithfulness and love, is seen as a foreshadow of Christ?

Our covenant with God

I came to faith in the Methodist Church and learned to value the New Year Covenant service where we renewed our commitment to Christ. Let me encourage you, as we near the end of this study of the book of Ruth, to make or renew your covenant to be a follower of the living God in the words of the Methodist service which contains an introduction (usually spoken by the minister) and then our response. Please only say those parts of this promise that you can honestly commit to. I pray that the example of Ruth and her covenantal pledge will be an encouragement to each of us.

> **Introduction**
> In the Old Covenant, God chose Israel to be his people and to obey his laws. Our Lord Jesus Christ, by his death and resurrection, has made a New Covenant with all who trust in him. We stand within this Covenant and we bear his name. On the one side, God promises in this Covenant to give us new life in Christ. On the other side, we are pledged to live no more for ourselves but for him.
> Beloved in Christ, let us again claim for ourselves this Covenant which God has made with his people, and take the yoke of Christ upon us. To take his yoke upon us means that we are content that he appoint us our place and work, and that he himself be our reward.

Christ has many services to be done; some are easy, others are difficult; some bring honour, others bring reproach; some are suitable to our natural inclinations and material interests, others are contrary to both. In some we may please Christ and please ourselves, in others we cannot please Christ except by denying ourselves. Yet the power to do all these things is given us in Christ, who strengthens us.
Therefore let us make the Covenant of God our own. Let us give ourselves anew to him, trusting in his promises and relying on his grace.

Response
Lord God, I am no longer my own, but yours. Put me to what you will, rank me with whom you will; put me to doing, put me to suffering; let me be employed by you or laid aside for you, exalted for you or brought low for you; let me be full, let me be empty; let me have all things, let me have nothing; I freely and wholeheartedly yield all things to your pleasure and disposal. And now, glorious and blessed God, Father, Son, and Holy Spirit, you are mine and I am yours. So be it. And the covenant now made on earth, let it be ratified in heaven.
Amen.

Signed: ________________________________

Date: ________________________________

Taken from *Methodist Worship Book*. Copyright © Trustees for Methodist Church purposes. Used by permission of Methodist Publishing House.

National Distributors

UK: (and countries not listed below)
CWR, Waverley Abbey House, Waverley Lane, Farnham, Surrey GU9 8EP.
Tel: (01252) 784700 Outside UK +44 1252 784700

AUSTRALIA: CMC Australasia, PO Box 519, Belmont, Victoria 3216.
Tel: (03) 5241 3288

CANADA: Cook Communications Ministries, PO Box 98, 55 Woodslee Avenue, Paris, Ontario.
Tel: 1800 263 2664

GHANA: Challenge Enterprises of Ghana, PO Box 5723, Accra.
Tel: (021) 222437/223249 Fax: (021) 226227

HONG KONG: Cross Communications Ltd, 1/F, 562A Nathan Road, Kowloon.
Tel: 2780 1188 Fax: 2770 6229

INDIA: Crystal Communications, 10-3-18/4/1, East Marredpalli, Secunderabad – 500026, Andhra Pradesh.
Tel/Fax: (040) 27737145

KENYA: Keswick Books and Gifts Ltd, PO Box 10242, Nairobi.
Tel: (02) 331692/226047 Fax: (02) 728557

MALAYSIA: Salvation Book Centre (M) Sdn Bhd, 23 Jalan SS 2/64, 47300 Petaling Jaya, Selangor.
Tel: (03) 78766411/78766797 Fax: (03) 78757066/78756360

NEW ZEALAND: CMC Australasia, PO Box 36015, Lower Hutt.
Tel: 0800 449 408 Fax: 0800 449 049

NIGERIA: FBFM, Helen Baugh House, 96 St Finbarr's College Road, Akoka, Lagos.
Tel: (01) 7747429/4700218/825775/827264

PHILIPPINES: OMF Literature Inc, 776 Boni Avenue, Mandaluyong City.
Tel: (02) 531 2183 Fax: (02) 531 1960

SINGAPORE: Armour Publishing Pte Ltd, Block 203A Henderson Road, 11–06 Henderson Industrial Park, Singapore 159546.
Tel: 6 276 9976 Fax: 6 276 7564

SOUTH AFRICA: Struik Christian Books, 80 MacKenzie Street, PO Box 1144, Cape Town 8000.
Tel: (021) 462 4360 Fax: (021) 461 3612

SRI LANKA: Christombu Books, 27 Hospital Street, Colombo 1.
Tel: (01) 433142/328909

TANZANIA: CLC Christian Book Centre, PO Box 1384, Mkwepu Street, Dar es Salaam.
Tel/Fax (022) 2119439

ZIMBABWE: Word of Life Books (Pvt) Ltd, Christian Media Centre, 8 Aberdeen Road, Avondale, PO Box A480, Harare, Zimbabwe. Tel: (04) 333355 or 091301188

For email addresses, visit the CWR website: www.cwr.org.uk

CWR is a Registered charity – Number 294387

CWR is a limited company registered in England – Registration Number 1990308

Day and Residential Courses
Counselling Training
Leadership Development
Biblical Study Courses
Regional Seminars
Ministry to Women
Daily Devotionals
Books and Videos
Conference Centre

Trusted all Over the World

CWR HAS GAINED A WORLDWIDE reputation as a centre of excellence for Bible-based training and resources. From our headquarters at Waverley Abbey House, Farnham, England, we have been serving God's people for 40 years with a vision to help apply God's Word to everyday life and relationships. The daily devotional *Every Day with Jesus* is read by nearly a million readers an issue in more than 150 countries, and our unique courses in biblical studies and pastoral care are respected all over the world. Waverley Abbey House provides a conference centre in a tranquil setting.

For free brochures on our seminars and courses, conference facilities, or a catalogue of CWR resources, please contact us at the following address.
CWR, Waverley Abbey House, Waverley Lane, Farnham, Surrey GU9 8EP, UK

Telephone: +44 (0)1252 784700
Email: mail@cwr.org.uk
Website: www.cwr.org.uk

CWR CRUSADE FOR WORLD REVIVAL
Applying God's Word to everyday life and relationships

Sing a New Song

Jeannette Barwick and Beverley Shepherd

Sing a New Song – The book of Psalms reflects the whole range of human emotions – from joy to despair, from praise to penitence, from trust to anxiety and from contentment to anger. This book explores seven of the psalms – songs of creation, redemption, delight, anger, protection, envy and thankfulness, each teaching us about a different aspect of God and how we might respond to Him. There are questions for reflection at the end of each chapter to help us explore the song we currently sing to God in the varying circumstances of our lives, and how we too can sing a new song!

£5.99 (plus p&p)

ISBN: 1-85345-366-8

Price correct at time of printing

Heart to Heart

Jeannette Barwick and Beverley Shepherd

The book's theme is that of the Lord's love for us – personal, unconditional and eternal. We are shown how to open ourselves to that love and to enter into a deeper relationship with Him.

£5.99 (plus p&p)

ISBN: 1-85345-311-0

Seasons of the Spirit

Jeannette Barwick and Beverley Shepherd

The focus of this book is to develop an awareness of what it means to move according to God's rhythm in our lives.

£5.99 (plus p&p)

ISBN: 1-85345-329-3

Prices correct at time of printing

Empowering Women

This book brings together contributions from respected Christian women, including Faith Forster, Mary Pytches and Ali Stibbe. These women share teaching and testimonies of God's call and the empowering of women as role models and encouragers to other women. 'When we join in God's plan, He refines and gifts and equips us.'

£6.99 (plus p&p)

ISBN: 1-85345-326-9

Price correct at time of printing